Praise for *The Loudest Duck*

"Laura Liswood has both great theoretical and practical understanding of diversity—why it is important in organizations and why attempts to create it often fail to deliver. *The Loudest Duck* is essential reading for anyone who wants to maximize the effectiveness of organizations or just wants to understand why things are the way they are."

—Rt. Hon. Kim Campbell
 Canada's 19th and first female Prime Minister

"Diversity is a popular buzzword, but too many organizations treat it as window dressing. Laura Liswood explains how successful leaders learn to value diversity for the advantages it brings. This book is clearly written, savvy, and wise."

—Joseph S. Nye Jr.
 University Distinguished Service Professor at Harvard University;
 Author of *The Powers to Lead*

"*The Loudest Duck* is a must read for managers and leaders of multinational corporations and international organizations. It provides an insightful look and fresh approach to cultural and gender differences that must be better understood for a more effective workplace."

—Ann M. Veneman
 Executive Director, UNICEF

"Laura Liswood brilliantly shows us how to get to Diversity 2.0 and beyond. A workplace of people from different backgrounds can lead to tensions, but this book shows, with great insights and examples, how it can lead to real creativity instead. It's an indispensable guide for managers and leaders—and also for anyone who wants to succeed in any aspect of life."

—Walter Isaacson
 President and Chief Executive Officer, The Aspen Institute

"Laura's timing is perfect and her message is spot on. Embracing diversity creates competitive advantage. Her book should be mandatory reading for everyone in business today. In the most engaging, fun, and real way, Laura gets to the heart of the opportunity—enabling Noah's diverse floating Ark to fly to the moon and beyond."

—Beth Brooke
 Global Vice Chair of Public Policy,
 Sustainability and Stakeholder Engagement, Ernst & Young

"Globalized businesses are increasingly aware that diversity belongs in the boardroom, not the public relations department, so *The Loudest Duck* is beautifully timed. Liswood is thoughtful and thought-provoking. Best of all, she's practical, helping ambitious employees from nondominant groups to prove their worth, and advising leaders how to transform diversity from rhetoric into an engine for innovation and growth."

—Kevin Kelley
  Chief Executive Officer, Heidrick & Struggles

"Iconoclastic and savvy, Laura Liswood's *The Loudest Duck* reminds us that not all diversities in the Ark are equal: Some in the Ark are louder and they get heard most. Combining an impressive breadth of research with colorful stories from corporate life, this book is essential reading for anyone who is serious about reaping the promise of diversity at work."

—Herminia Ibarra
  Professor of Organizational Behavior
  The Cora Chaired Professor of Leadership and Learning
  Director, INSEAD Leadership Initiative

"Brilliant! Liswood offers unique insight and fresh tools for a Diversity 2.0 world. Drawing on thinkers from Thucydides to Malcolm Gladwell, and on more than three decades of executive experience, she offers leaders ideas for building a meritocracy that will ensure corporate success."

—Robin Gerber
  Author of *Leadership the Eleanor Roosevelt Way*
  and *Barbie and Ruth*

"*The Loudest Duck* is one of the clearest and most profoundly informative analyses of why, despite decades of effort and investment, most diversity initiatives fail to produce the promised benefits to organizations or their employees. This book goes beyond analysis and provides a new language of metaphor that captures the unexamined dynamics of dominance, unearned privilege, and unconscious bias that undermine our attempts to create truly diverse and inclusive workplaces.

   In her introduction Laura Liswood makes clear her goal to move us beyond Diversity 1.0. She is successful. The Loudest Duck has the potential to usher in Diversity 2.0, a new conversation and approach to changing our organizations and ourselves. It is a must reading for leaders who are serious about diversity and inclusion in their organizations."

—David A. Thomas
  H. Naylor Fitzhugh Professor of Business Administration,
  Harvard Business School
  Author of *Breaking Through: The Making of Minority Executives in Corporate America*

the
Loudest
Duck

the Loudest Duck

Moving Beyond Diversity
While Embracing Differences
TO
Achieve Success at Work

Laura Liswood

WILEY

John Wiley & Sons, Inc.

Published by John Wiley & Sons, Inc., Hoboken, New Jersey.
Published simultaneously in Canada.

For general information on our other products and services or for technical support, please contact our Customer Care Department within the United States at (800) 762-2974, outside the United States at (317) 572-3993 or fax (317) 572-4002.

Wiley also publishes its books in a variety of electronic formats. Some content that appears in print may not be available in electronic books. For more information about Wiley products, visit our web site at www.wiley.com.

ISBN 978-0-470-48584-2

Printed in the United States of America.

10

To my sister, Jan

Contents

Acknowledgments

I have been incredibly fortunate in my career and life to have many people take an interest in the work I do and who have shared the same passion I have about leadership. So many have reached out and boosted me along the journey.

My work has benefitted from women and men who live brave, courageous, curious, spirited lives, and have spent their lives wanting to change and improve the world.

They are a diverse lot and I honor them.

Perhaps most fortunate in my path, I have been able to work for and with an extraordinary group of people around the world. I could not have imagined that I would call friends Vigdis Finnbogadottir, former President of Iceland; Kim Campbell, former Prime Minister of Canada; and Mary Robinson, former President of Ireland. Each of them has guided and cared about me, the work of leadership, and that of the Council of Women World Leaders.

Goldman Sachs is an exceptional organization filled with gifted and talented people. I have worked with and been supported by so many, it is difficult to know where to start. I must acknowledge and thank Edith Hunt, a superb manager and thinker on issues of human capital, diversity, and much beyond. Lloyd Blankfein, Chairman of Goldman Sachs, chaired the original diversity committee at the firm and he really sets the standard for the organization and for its management. He also taught me that humor goes a long way. Edith Cooper, Kevin Kennedy, John Rogers, Esta Stecher, Sarah Smith, Abby Joseph Cohen, Carol Pledger, Aynesh Johnson, Lucas Van Praag, Donna Fisher, Bob Hormats, and Steve Kerr are just some who make Goldman Sachs so unique and in the forefront of the challenges facing global and diverse companies.

I must thank Robin Gerber for her constant upbeat energy and marketing savvy. My agents, Howard Yoon and Gail Ross, continue to believe in my work and to support my seemingly endless efforts. Melinda Wolfe, Kimberley Bentley, Clarissa Bonde are great allies, and friends. Adrienne Arsht, who "but for" her belief in my work on women leaders, I would never have gone down this path. The Aspen Institute, under Walter Isaacson, has been an intellectual home. And to the Honorable Jane Herman, Director, CEO, and President, Woodrow Wilson International Center for Scholars, thank you for your dedication to women's leadership.

Leaders who have been especially generous with their time and their help, their experience and wisdom include Joseph Nye, Jr., David Gergen, Laura Tyson, Christine Di Stefano (who has been there since the beginning), Harinder Kohli, Janet Napolitano, Cherie Blair, Pepper Schwartz, Heather Wilson, Gwen Ifil, Madeleine Albright, Ellen Johnson-Sirleaf, and Margot Wallstrom.

Edited interviews with some of these leaders can be found on the book's website www.theloudestduck.com.

Thanks must also be given to Klaus Schwab, the visionary leader who conceived of the World Economic Forum, and Saadia Zahidi, who have given me the gift of a seat at the table and an unparalleled view of the world.

To the men and women of the Washington, DC Metropolitan Police Department, you are my heroes.

Special thanks to the scholars, researchers, and writers in the field of diversity including Deborah Tannen, Judith Rosner, Kim Campbell, DebbieWalsh, Anna Fels, Ilene Lang, Melanne Verveer, Linda Babcock, Richard Fox, Sylvia Ann Hewlett, David Thomas, Pippa Norris, Herminia Ibarra, Beth Brooke, Iris Bohnet, Amanda Ellis, Barbara Lee, Patricia Deyton, and many more great thinkers doing work on this important part of leadership.

To my family of relatives and friends, two-footed and four-footed, thank you for your support. Thank you to, among many others, Linda and Caitlin, Melody and Candace, Mel S., Tom, Amy and Richard, Carol and Bob, Bruce and Susan, my mother Dorothy, the Hartmans, Deborah and Ann, Laurie and Jan E., Lew, Michael, Kim, and Hershey, and the ever-purring Mao. You always encourage my efforts, listen patiently to my complaints, and gently suggest—you are so important to me. And to my sister Jan, I miss you.

Finally, no book is an island. Alina Dumitrasc of the Council of Women World Leaders supports me fully, and Bridget Samburg was crucial to the book's creation and a powerful voice to me. Ashley Allison, Christine Moore, Peter Knox, Analise Siciliano, Linda Indig, and especially my editor, Dan Ambrosio of John Wiley & Sons, kept the energy high, got it from the beginning, and knew which Duck to choose.

All mistakes, errors, and omissions are mine alone.

Introduction

My corporate career has spanned more than 20 years, and in that time I have seen firsthand how valiantly companies have tried to establish greater diversity and equality among their employees. The trend and recognition of the importance of diversity has grown, particularly as the world becomes more closely linked and we work more often with people who are not like us.

Unfortunately, many of the diversity initiatives have been successful on paper, but not in practice. They often ascribe to what I call the Noah's ark theory of diversity. If you bring two of every kind aboard an organization then you've solved the problem—except you really haven't. After all, we are all products of our life experiences and upbringings, and we all bring our whole selves into the workplace. Too often, the mere mention of diversity results in collective eye rolling. It is seen as an annoyance, a lowering of standards, a thorn in a company's side, a necessary obligatory part of the mission statement. Diversity has earned itself a bad name since many people think it gives advantage to particular groups. Diversity isn't the problem. The problem is that we all bring our unconscious beliefs about ourselves and who others are into the workplace. The more diverse the workplace, the more likely it is we won't have a fair and level playing field, not because of the diversity, but because of how we treat those who are different from ourselves.

If you want to create more diversity, you can't just play the numbers game. You have to shape the attitudes and tendencies of people in the organization, from the top down and the bottom up. You have to foster an environment free of subtle advantages and subtle disadvantages so that all employees work on a fair and level playing field. You can't just throw a team of corporate animals together and expect them to get along. You can't expect to evaluate them without any of the unconscious perceptions you bring. Instead, you have to build awareness of the dynamics of difference and you must do this consciously.

Today, a shift in the composition of corporate power is taking place. American dominance is being torn apart by the forces of globalization and financial upheaval. Small cracks in the traditional white male hierarchy are giving way to a rich texture of different voices, different cultures, and the demands injected by market forces that are ebbing and flowing across national boundaries. Lately, women and other historically out-of-power groups have emerged as major players in economic development and decision making at all levels.

In this new century, an overwhelming number of Fortune 500 companies do business overseas and are considered global. Even the smallest company is likely to have interests in expanding markets. For companies with global markets, the workplace today is an intricate tapestry of multilingual, multicultural, and multistylistic threads. Diversity has become a given, but we will see that these diverse workplaces present unique challenges which most organizations have yet to overcome.

Diversity—true diversity—requires changes in unconscious attitudes. I have seen firsthand how difficult it is for a company to raise the sea level of its workplace and reap the real benefits of diversity. To start, it is important to be aware that in all social and work settings there are dominant and nondominant groups. By dominant, I am referring to a person or entity historically in power or over-represented in highly prized positions. This is a group, or person, who feels entitled to assume this role or feels they obtained the position in a fair way. They may also receive subtle advantages without being conscious of them. Non-dominant groups are historically underrepresented in the world's hierarchy of power; individuals from these groups may face subtle disadvantages and preconceived attitudes and beliefs from the dominant group. They may have less of a sense of entitlement to their rightful place. In addition, they will have to navigate the workplace in a different way than the dominant group.

In the American office space, the most identifiable dominant group is men, and usually white men. The easiest nondominant groups to spot are women and minorities, but the distinctions between dominant and nondominant do not stop there. Noah's ark is full of different groups. There can be divisions in the office between tall and short people, fat and thin, straight and gay, extroverts and introverts, and even between Red Sox and Yankees fans. We bring our unconscious beliefs about every group, taught to us in a variety of ways as we grew up. This is why we must go *beyond diversity*, and why creating a successful Noah's ark presents significant—but not insurmountable—challenges. Turns out though it is a lot harder than we originally thought.

I became acutely aware of the role of dominant and nondominant groups many years ago while working for a financial institution, when I was asked to help conduct an internal corporate study on issues of fairness in the workplace. We talked to four groups: white American men, white American women, minorities, and non-Americans. The good news? One of the groups thought the organization was a meritocracy. Three of the groups did not walk in the same world as the dominant group, and therefore did not experience their workplace as meritocratic. It didn't necessarily make the dominant group uncaring, unthinking, or biased; they merely assumed their experiences were the same as others.

Not surprisingly, I found that many women felt stuck inside an old–boys' network. They complained that promotions and raises favored their male coworkers, especially if they were white. Ethnic and racial minorities, meanwhile, complained that they weren't being seen or heard as much as their colleagues. They felt like poster children for diversity and a way to deflect legal challenges; they were the token Indian, Chinese, or Latino on the corporate ark.

Most white men—the dominant power group—well-intentioned and capable, were surprised to hear their colleagues' observations, and didn't think their views had merit since this was clearly not what they had experienced. This was not a bad intention on their part. They just believed, because they expected it more than any other group, that their company indeed functioned as a meritocracy. They were confident that hard work pays off, and that the salary and promotions were handed out fairly and justly. In hindsight, their perspective comes as no surprise. If you are at the top of the corporation's hierarchy, it's not likely that you would say to yourself, "The reason I am at the top is that I have been subtly advantaged, and all of those others have been subtly disadvantaged." In fact, you would probably believe just the opposite and think, "I got to the top because my company is a meritocracy and fair and only the best rise up the ladder. I am one of the best and have proven myself over time."

Many years have passed since that internal corporate study. During those years, I worked with businesses and corporate and political leaders to better understand the subject of diversity and why I believe we must move beyond our traditional thinking. We need to get beyond the bricks and mortar of diversity as we know it—the committees, the employee networks, and the trainings. The lawyer in me says these are all necessary, but not sufficient. That is Diversity 1.0. Now we need to move to Diversity 2.0. This is the purpose of *The Loudest Duck*.

Mary Catherine Bateson, anthropologist and president of the Institute for Intercultural Studies, believes that life is a meandering journey, especially for women. She says women often find that "things happened" rather than resulting from some premeditated trajectory and career. In her book, *Composing a Life*, Bateson talks about how this approach to one's life is unique to women as we often find ourselves in places that we didn't imagine initially.

My path to The *Loudest Duck* feels composed much in this meandering way. I did not start out with this book in mind. Rather, it happened, and I ended up here, with this need to go beyond diversity. I suspect my interest in thinking about the world of difference we live in started when I was a law student doing work on Title VII class-action suits at a law firm in Sacramento, California. Title VII basically prohibits discrimination based on a number of categories, including gender. In 1973, I was working on behalf of a woman who was suing a newspaper because the "help wanted" ads were still categorized according to gender. I was astounded that the company responsible for the ads could still be operating with such an outdated mental framework. This was more than nine years after the law prohibited this sort of division. I was baffled why no one from the homogeneous management team of the organization being sued thought this was a problem.

Throughout my career in business, I have often felt what I call *disappeared*, and I came to learn that many of my female colleagues did too. We just weren't being *seen* or *heard* in the same way that the men were. Our impact and presence seemed muted in comparison, but my eyes were opened even further when an African American woman told me that she felt as though flight attendants on airplanes often looked right past her. They didn't *see* her. She described sitting on a plane, on multiple occasions, and having flight attendants overlook her when taking drink orders. To not be seen, I concluded, didn't just happen to women; it happened to those who were not in the dominant group, whatever that group might be.

Later in my career, after law school and business school, I became a senior examiner for the Malcolm Baldrige National Quality Award, a prestigious national award presented by the National Institute of Standards and Technology to the highest quality companies. I learned how powerful leadership could be in creating the values and actions that shape people and organizations. Conscious leadership actually does matter. This led me to try to understand what it is that creates great leaders in both men and women and what impact these individuals can have on others. What traits do great leaders have? I wondered.

Psychologist and Harvard professor Howard Gardner's book on leadership, *Leading Minds*, led me further down this path of inquiry and examination. I was intrigued by Gardner's view that great leaders have four traits, which I summarize as the following:

1. A "True North" that serves as an internal compass of values
2. The willingness to challenge authority
3. The practical skills to communicate to others
4. The ability to travel outside their own worldview

These are still the traits I use to examine leadership and successful individual leaders. This framework, coupled with innovative research from the Center for American Woman and Politics at Rutgers University, kicked my mental can further down the road. The center's research finds that women state legislators legislate differently than men. Women apparently interact with constituents differently, speak in committee meetings differently, and introduce different bills than men.

My thoughts meandered further. If this was true for women legislators, what might happen if a woman became President of the United States? Would something be different in how she led the country? To even begin to answer that question I had to go outside the United States, since as a nation we have yet to put a woman in the White House. In 1994 there were 15 women, still living, who were or had been president or prime minister of a country. I wanted to know the secret, the key to whether there was something different about a female head of state or government. I needed to understand how such differences were revealed. I set out to see if *I* could interview one of them. I had no idea why I thought I could meet a woman president or prime minister. I am not Barbara Walters, not from CNN, and I've never interviewed anyone to ask them what kind of a tree they would be if they were a tree. I did have some fear about stepping out of my comfort zone, but a few years previously, I had bicycled across Siberia and on the Marco Polo Silk Route through Uzbekistan, Kyrgyzstan, Kazakhstan, China, and Pakistan. The overriding emotion while doing that was fear, but I had to learn just to live with it or I wouldn't have been able to do the grueling trips.

I did learn a big lesson through my interviews with world leaders.

Much to my surprise and 18 months later, I had met all of the women presidents and prime ministers. Each one agreed to meet with me and no one turned me down. Admittedly, Margaret Thatcher told me to come back to her once I had met everyone else! I am an experiential learner so in truth I was eternally grateful that I had met 14 other presidents and prime ministers before meeting with Thatcher. I realized also that if I had never asked for the interviews, the answer would have been no, but by asking, the possibility was a yes.

Those interviews were instrumental in my under-standing of how difference is much more difficult for us to embrace than we might think. Most of the world's women leaders said they were treated differently from their male colleagues. This manifested itself in many ways, from how the press scrutinized them and the level of tolerance for their mistakes, to ways in which these women had to change their communication styles in order to be heard.

Margaret Thatcher was once told that women's voices often rise at the end of sentences, as if a question is being asked. This is something, she learned, that doesn't happen with men's voices. Through her groundbreaking work on female and male communication styles, Deborah Tannen would explain that the rise in the voice is a relational technique and a pattern of ritual modesty that women learn at a young age. When told that men hear a lack of confidence when women speak this way, it is said that Lady Thatcher went to a speech coach to learn to drop this inflection so that she could sound more like a man, and in turn be heard by men. She speaks in the ritual way that men speak, as I share with you later in the book.

Rosabeth Moss Kanter, holder of the Ernest L. Arbuckle Professorship at Harvard Business School, says that if you are the only "O" in a room full of "X"s, your choices are limited and often all you can do is try to turn yourself into an "X". There is a risk inherent in doing so though. As I discuss later in the book, women who transform from the "O" to the "X" may end up being considered too aggressive. It's a delicate balancing act in a diverse organization.

My time spent with female leaders around the globe grew into the creation of the Council of Women World Leaders, of which I am Secretary General. I also co-founded an organization (with Barbara Lee and Marie Wilson) called The White House Project, the mission of which is to assist in electing a woman to political office who could eventually assume the position of United States Commander in Chief. The Council and this effort are focused around developing women as some of the most powerful, skilled leaders in the world. The Project works to overcome stereotypes and boundaries, all while looking at why and how people resist differences.

My life took another bend in the road on September 11, 2001. I was in New York City's financial district, not far from the World Trade Center, when the planes went into the towers. In the midst of the tragedy, I found that I wanted to become trained as a First Responder to help others. I was devastated by the events and by my own lack of control and inability to help anyone. I was over 53 at the time and in what can only be considered an age-defying moment, I spent 10 months in the Washington, DC Police Academy and became a reserve police officer. I like to say that I became the oldest living female police mountain bike officer. I was later promoted to sergeant.

This opportunity has opened up an entirely new world for me and provided me with a new and different perspective. I work with people from varying socioeconomic levels, education backgrounds, and life experiences. My command structure is predominantly African American. All of this is very different from my exposure to typical corporate life. Ironically, some of what I now bring into my work in the corporate world, I learned at the police academy. I often discuss and employ a technique I learned from my police training called Verbal Judo. I have become more conscious of my actions and more aware of how I speak and the danger of unconscious speaking, thinking, and acting in the workplace when you are faced with diversity.

I thought my journey was strictly about gender, but it became clear to me that this is more about dominant and nondominant cultures. My questions, curiosities, and desires to find solutions centered on the diversity inherent in the dominant cultures and nondominant cultures and what creates truly fair workplaces. I became intrigued by how these nondominant groups were adapting to or adjusting for the dominance. They must adapt or else they will fail. I realized that what is true for the nondominant woman in any culture might also be true for the Japanese man who becomes nondominant when faced with the kind of athletic, macho style that permeates Western culture in many organizations and institutions.

I began to understand that, ironically, it is NOT the diversity that is the problem. It is the unconscious handling of diversity that creates the lack of fairness in the organization. It is not the fault of the diverse, nondominant groups nor is it the fault of the homogeneous dominant groups in power. It is that diverse organizations require more sophisticated leadership, conscious awareness, thought, behavior, and tools to reap the benefits of what true diversity can provide.

I have been extremely fortunate to work for Goldman Sachs, first as the managing director for Global Leadership and Diversity and now as a senior advisor. The company has an unerring focus on this mission. It understands in a way I've found few other companies do that diversity is far more complex than many in leadership would have thought. They have not been satisfied with Diversity 1.0 but are keenly aware of the journey they are on by committing large resources of money, management commitment, strategic thinking, and time. I have honed my own thinking and perspective on going beyond diversity through my work with Goldman Sachs.

All of which brings me to *The Loudest Duck*. The old ways of thinking about diversity are just that—old. The approaches to accepting, tolerating, embracing, including, incorporating, and benefiting from difference are more nuanced than we once thought. Really benefitting from diversity is a complex but richly rewarding mission! This book challenges the old frameworks in order to move us to the next level of awareness and action when it comes to difference. As we continue to conduct our lives with difference, through different lenses, we need to adopt a new understanding of diversity. We need a new vision, new approaches, and new goals. The tools, frameworks, and parables in this book offer a new vision, and a new opportunity to embrace and capitalize on the differences that are actually assets in our global workplace. Difference in the workplace and in society is no longer simply something we tolerate or even embrace. We are beyond that. But our mind-set is still stuck in diversity as we once knew it. We must move beyond. It is my hope that after you read *The Loudest Duck* you will have another view of the world, a different perspective, and that you will discover more tools to succeed in the workplace today and tomorrow. It is my hope that you too will compose your life a bit differently.

And the title *The Loudest Duck*? Keep reading.

Chapter 1

Beware of Noah's Ark

Two women, two Asians, two people with disabilities, and two African Americans: diversity accomplished — or so we once thought. At some point, corporate diversity came to mean the inclusion of at least *two of every kind*. Far too many managers and leaders figured that if you crammed a pair of each minority into a company or into a boardroom, you had accomplished the task of creating a diverse work environment.

Nothing, in fact, could be further from reality. We've thought long and erroneously that diversity was achieved merely by re-creating Noah's ark. At least, that's how the thinking has gone. The push for diversity came to be about numbers, committees, employee networks, and mission statements; strategic plans, tracking systems, business cases, and scorecards. It's true that in Noah's ark, those might all be necessary; but we've come to find that they are not sufficient.

The problem with this artificial ark is that much of the time, the giraffe looks at the zebra and thinks—consciously or unconsciously—"That animal is just kind of funny looking. He doesn't look like me. He has a foolishly short neck, silly black and white stripes, and eats what looks like garbage. However, as a giraffe, I have an elegant long neck, beautiful brown and white spots, and eat carefully; only the finest leaves and bark." And that's just the beginning of how all of these creatures see each other. The gazelle inevitably thinks that the hippo is ridiculously fat and lazy; the leopard finds the stripes on the tiger jarring; the rabbits and the coyotes can't be in the same room together; and the racket the magpies make during the day incenses the nocturnal owls.

This is what happens when you create the corporate version of Noah's ark; and such clashes will happen indefinitely until leaders and companies come up with a plan for integrating these groups, and benefiting from the stripes, the spots, and the horns rather than waiting for company-wide conformity. It will continue to take place until everyone in the workplace learns and understands that their own inherent behaviors and unconscious approaches are likely hindering success for everyone. In a true meritocracy, the benefit of diversity will emerge only when we become aware and conscious of how we feel about the *other* who is sharing our space in the ark. It will occur when we become aware of the subtle ways in which some in the ark are advantaged while others are disadvantaged—merely because of their diversity. Only then can we understand how the beliefs, roles, shoulds, should nots, values, schemas, and archetypes that we bring into the workplace affect one another.

In the United States, the corporate Noah's ark still has only 13 female CEOs running the largest 500 publicly traded companies—that's a record. In 1996 there was a mere one female CEO of a Fortune 500 company; in 2008 there were 11. As for African American men, there are four currently running a Fortune 500 company. This book isn't all about gender or race, but this will give you an idea of how far we haven't come and how far we still have to go.

Journalist James Surowiecki captures an important point about diversity in his book, *The Wisdom of Crowds*. He says that what we are really looking for is "cognitive diversity," or the differing ways people think. He explains that if you have a homogeneous group and you add an additional member of the homogeneous group to the mix, the individuals will bond quickly because they are alike—but the incremental creativity between them is slight. If you add a member of the heterogeneous group to the homogeneous one, they do *not* bond quickly, because although they are not alike, the incremental creativity is much greater when each group reaches its full potential. Companies are ultimately looking for increased creativity, better ideas, and multiple perspectives, so they will in fact benefit from diversity. However, we will see that achieving this takes much more effort than merely assembling a workplace that looks like Noah's ark.

We now need to move beyond diversity. Gone are the days of traditional diversity training—something that ultimately proved to be ineffective. We have to look at companies and employees in a new postdiversity way. A review of 830 mid- to large-sized companies around the United States found that typical diversity training exercises were followed by a 7.5 percent drop in the number of women in management. The number of female African American managers fell by 10 percent, while the number of male African Americans dropped by 12 percent. This study—examined by the *Washington Post* in "Most Diversity Training Ineffective, Study Finds"—revealed that mandatory diversity training programs were the culprits. Trainings that concerned diversity were found to be more effective when they were voluntary and used to achieve specific company goals.

Businesses in the United States collectively spend between $200 and $300 million each year on diversity training; yet all that time and money could be spent more effectively to achieve more productive results. We are asking people within a diverse population to change their unconscious thoughts, beliefs, schemas, perceptions, role types, and behaviors, while acting more consciously among and around others who are not like them. It makes existence in heterogeneous workplaces more complex, and it makes fair career success more challenging. Changes in perceptions and beliefs about ourselves and others in the ark are required, and we all know that people are reluctant to change. It can be scary, uncertain, and uncomfortable. Successful and effective change starts with the unthinkable, moves to the impossible, and ends with the inevitable. But too often, we become stuck in the unthinkable.

Ancient Roman historian Cornelius Tacitus said, "The worst crimes were dared by a few, willed by more and accepted by all." The same goes for change; a small group dares it before more join in and ultimately it is accepted by everyone. A standing ovation is a classic metaphor for change. Typically, an initial but small number of people jump up to yell "bravo"; then another larger group stands believing that the performance was especially worthwhile; followed by an even larger crowd that gets up, believing that the performance was good based on how others are receiving it. Finally, the people remaining in their seats stand up because they can't see the stage and have no other choice.

People need to realize that creating diverse environments is, in effect, all about change. This is inherently difficult to grasp. There has historically been more resistance than acceptance to these changes. None of us feel excited and happy when we see competition, threats to our job, challenges to our thinking, or creativity that surpasses our own. These can be scary things, but change can be less painful than we think. Another ancient philosopher, Thucydides, observed that people end up changing for three reasons: out of fear, self-interest, or honor. I like to think of these, in modern terms, as pain, gain, or vision. I may change because it is too painful to stay the way I am. I may even change because it is clear that I will gain from the change. Least likely, I will change because I have the vision to understand that it is in everyone's best interest for me to change.

Once we've assembled Noah's ark, we can't stop there. That is merely Diversity 1.0. We must go to the next level and require ourselves to be more conscious about our actions and decisions while changing—if not at first adjusting—our perspectives, beliefs, and most importantly, our behaviors in the workplace. A successful corporate Noah's ark is a lot harder to achieve than we imagine, because there are far more categories of difference, or diversity, that trigger our unconscious reactions. The categories extend beyond the traditionally defined distinctions that include age, race, gender, national origin, and religion. Try to discern the myriad unconscious assumptions we make about personal characteristics such as marital status, family structure, sexual orientation, belief systems, height, weight, accent, hobbies, sports, country of origin, class, smoking habits, food preferences, personality approaches, gradations of skin color, and speaking styles. These are all distinct types found on the ark. True diversity requires that we tackle these subtle and unique categories head on. Each one must be incorporated into the ark and into the corporate composition. Yet, it is challenging to overcome our own natural or learned perceptions of each of these groups, because we learn about others starting at an early age, and this learning continues throughout our lives.

Let's look at who is in this ark I keep mentioning. The issue as we look inside the ark isn't merely that difference *exists*, but rather that we *evaluate* people unconsciously. This can have a real impact in the workplace on promotions, salaries, and performance metrics. It can disturb the professional playing field, *not* because of the diversity in the ark, but because of how we respond to individuals who are different than we are. Some specific examples follow. This is not an exhaustive list by any means.

National Origin. We may be pleased that our company has hired people from various countries of origin, but we should really be focusing on how everyone is reacting to each other. We can use a word like *nationality*, but what this really means is that people have their own notions or ideas about each other's country of origin. What do the French really think of the English? What do we do about the Japanese attitude toward the Chinese? What about the ways in which Italians view Germans? If you ask someone their honest opinion regarding national origins, you are sure to hear quite a commentary, quite a host of assumptions, predictions, and decisions. Germans are too stolid and too unemotional, think the Italians. Italians are much too emotional, heated, and dramatic, think the Germans. Herein lies the Noah's ark challenge.

Age. It is not so much that age is an issue, a problem, or an obstacle, but rather that we have to be aware of what we unconsciously believe about what 20-year-olds can do, what 40-year-olds are capable of, and what 60-year-olds are really all about. We may believe that the millennial generation or 20-somethings are unfocused, not particularly loyal to one organization, and have short attention spans. Don't even try to give them critical feedback, since those helicopter parents of theirs never did. Many have decided that millennials use electronic media such as Facebook in a way that dissolves the lines between personal and professional, and we probably don't like it. But we are doing an individual a disservice, our company harm, and ourselves unnecessary angst by forming these judgments about the 20-something who was just hired. It's not uncommon to assume that the 55-year-old is stuck in her ways and unwilling to make adjustments. Maybe she is, but maybe she isn't.

Culture. This really boils down to how we live in the world and how that may be different from another person's way of being or doing things. Our cultural differences are often labeled as weird or strange, rather than viewed as merely not the same as our own. "You eat that part of the animal?" we think to ourselves watching someone savor a particular organ. Maybe we're judging our colleagues because they kiss each cheek when greeting someone, or hold hands. "That's so not right," we think. Nor is that little ritual we saw before a meal, the small bow to a superior, or a phrase used for greeting someone that isn't "Hello." It's hard not to think, "We don't do that here." In order to make Noah's ark work, more of us have to accept that what we do *here* isn't what we've always done, and if it's different it doesn't necessarily mean it's bad. That's cultural difference in a microcosm.

Religion. If we share the same religion as another person, then we have a sense of each other's values in terms of what, where, why, whom, and when we believe. In turn, we are comfortable in the knowledge that we understand one another. To know is to understand, to feel comfortable, to feel right, and to feel okay about our cubicle neighbor, our supervisor, or our newly hired charge. If we don't share the same religion, we really do not understand each other very well. Our value system—and certainly our rituals—may be different. It may not be a clash of civilizations, but it is a clash of unconscious understandings that quickly plays out in the workplace.

Say, for instance, that your boss likes to take people out for drinks on Fridays after work as a team bonding experience. Immediately this seemingly thoughtful, spirited gesture includes certain people and excludes others. Jews who observe the Sabbath or Muslims who do not drink and may be uncomfortable in a bar setting are automatically excluded. And this doesn't take into consideration the person who has adult- or child-care responsibilities. So a manager's perfectly good impulse to create a strong team and get familiar with her colleagues turns into a subtle advantage for those who participate, and a subtle disadvantage for others in Noah's ark who are not out for drinks at the end of the week. What are the effects of this potentially unequal treatment? The ones who go out with the manager have unequal access to the manager—the same person who ultimately makes career decisions about others naturally and unconsciously leans toward the people he or she has become comfortable with after hours.

Holidays are another factor. If we share the same religion, we know each other's holidays—including the dates, the celebrations, and the meanings. You'd have to have been born in a cave not to know about Christmas in the Western world, and I'm sure you've casually wished many people a Merry Christmas. But what about the 1.5 billion Muslims who celebrate the holiday of Ramadan, which is less known in many places around the world, and not even acknowledged in some.

Gender. What do we bring to our place of work that we learned long ago about gender—about men and women? Ben Barres tells of an experience that he had as a transgender individual. Barres—who went from being a female to being a male—discusses a science presentation he made after which he overheard a male scientist say, "Ben gave a great seminar today, but his work is much better than his sister's work." The male scientist had initially seen

Ben give his presentation as a female. I am sure that although much had changed about Ben, his scientific research hadn't. This man had brought his unconscious way of hearing, thinking, and perceiving to the lecture. Men gave better presentations, in his opinion. As a male, Ben says that he is also interrupted much less often than when he was a female.

Sexual Orientation. It may depend upon what our belief system has taught us, or what our parents said, or how our childhood peers informed us, but we all come to the table with a set of ideas on how we think about gays, lesbians, bisexuals, and the transgendered. We may be less comfortable talking to the woman who is married to another woman when we're looking for a colleague with whom to bounce ideas around. A male supervisor may have decided—as many men do—that his gay project manager will think he's hitting on him for suggesting the two get lunch to talk over some strategies for an upcoming presentation. Therefore, the supervisor falls back to relying on the person who is more like him, altogether missing out on hearing from those particular employees.

A manager may not really get to know an employee who is gay through casual postweekend chitchat. A simple question such as, "What did you do this weekend?" may never transpire. Likewise, when assumptions are made about sexual orientation, a gay employee who is not "out" may end up avoiding questions—stumbling through seemingly simple exchanges about weekend plans and end up not connecting at all—in an effort to hide his identity. This becomes a missed opportunity for an employee and manager to bond over small things, and ultimately that manager will be influenced by the lack of those small, pleasant exchanges. In the end, decisions are based on both conscious and unconscious knowledge, which leaves some with a significant advantage and others with a clear disadvantage.

Socioeconomics or Class. This category crosses over many cultural, racial, and religious boundaries. Think about how class affects perceptions of who people are, and what they are capable of achieving. We all have an internal compass about class; it's one category that quickly separates the haves from the have-nots. Elite blacks, whites, Chileans, and Chinese, for example, can often find common humor, talk about similar cars, homes, or vacations, and may have similar preferences in the arts. This is the phenomenon known as "Davos Man," and is a commonality based on class, not geography. Money divides like nothing else. Often when I am in India and ask about the different categories of diversity in the company ark, one of the first responses is *caste*—a word that would be unthinkable in many other places globally, but quite prevalent there in unconscious and conscious thought.

I once asked a company director to explain the dress code in the company. The answer was simple for him in his world; he told me that it was "country-club casual." I come from a blue-collar background, and my father was a policeman. I've long been working in the white-collar world, but my first exposure to country-club dress codes came when I waited on tables and picked up golf balls at the club near where I grew up. Without those jobs, I wouldn't have been able to decipher country-club casual. For employees from other countries and class backgrounds, this is useless information that reflects a certain unaware, insider mind-set.

Take another example of two people interviewing for a position in the same organization. One candidate comes from a well-to-do family and is accustomed to reading the *New York Times* every day. While he was growing up, his parents invited interesting people to dinner who spoke about politics, current events, and literature. This person was able to travel abroad for a year during college because his parents could afford it. They also hired a language and calculus tutor for him. These same parents also belong to a private dining club, so the candidate learned early on how to dine in fine restaurants—the sort that are set with multiple forks, spoons, and knives. One of the parents went to the same college as the candidate, and that parent had donated a large sum to the alumni campaign. (According to *The Economist*, legacy students are two to four times more likely to get into a school than their equally qualified competitor who is without a legacy.)

The second candidate—who had the same grades in college and the same degrees—comes to the organization for an interview from a family that was headed by a single parent who worked two jobs. The candidate had to spend summers watching her siblings during the day. Study time had to be squeezed in at the school library during school hours, or not at all. She worked weekends and evenings to defray tuition. She had no year abroad, no stimulating dinner table conversation, *New York Times*, tutors, or lessons in salad forks; just plain hard work, gut-felt ambition, and a desire to better herself.

The company recruiter may well be unconsciously looking for someone more like the first candidate than the second one, because there is a subtle and unconscious question being asked, which is, "Who is more like me?" It's probably clear to you at this point who has the unconscious advantage here. The playing field between these two candidates is uneven in a subtle and unconscious way. The recruiter is not specifically biased, but he is more comfortable with someone to whom he can relate. And in the end—when the grades and the degrees on paper are the same—there is still an intuitive instinct that remains. That gut may well favor the first candidate if he looks like the recruiter. Like is comfortable with like.

Ironically, another possibility is that the recruiter may in fact hire the second person precisely because she is different, and the recruiter has been challenged to hire for difference. But if the organization is not actually ready for the difference, and has not gone beyond Noah's ark, it will be a fruitless hire. At a meeting with diversity experts, I was struck by the following anonymous quote, which I explore in Chapter 6: "We hire for difference and then we fire because they aren't the same."

Marital Status. Almost all of us have an unconscious reaction to the marital status of our colleagues. Maybe we judge someone because they are divorced, assume the 43-year-old unmarried male must have commitment issues, or wonder why the 20-something woman got married so young. She must be insecure or need a man, we assume. Barbara Mikulski, a United States senator from Maryland, has a humorous take on this. She says, "If you are a woman with a career, a high-powered position, and you are *single*, people think that you couldn't get a husband because you are working so hard. If you are a *married* woman with a high-powered career, people may evaluate you and think you must be neglecting your husband because of your career. If you are *divorced* with that career, it is pretty clear that your career was a priority and you drove your husband away. And finally, if you are a *widow* with that high-powered career; well, you must have killed him." We judge and assume, and end up missing out on the more important (and verifiable) merits of our employees or our colleagues.

Family. One of the biggest beasts on the corporate Noah's ark is the white elephant known as family status. Children or no children? In the workplace, the topic of kids makes people positively squeamish. There is the uncertainty about whether your employees have kids, or whether your new hire is thinking about starting a family. That is often the unspoken million-dollar question in the workplace. Maybe this has happened to you, or maybe you can just imagine being a manager and having a woman come to you with a few simple words that immediately become not so simple. "I'm pregnant," she says. After the obligatory "Oh, congratulations!" what truly goes through your mind as a manager? Probably a litany of questions, such as, When is she leaving? Who will take over her work while she is gone? When is she coming back? When—and if—she does come back, what will that be like? Will she need special hours and flexible work time? While none of these questions are unreasonable, all this woman did was tell you she's pregnant, and in a snap you've come up with an impossibly long list of questions, many of which border on judgments.

I once asked a man who had sat through one of my presentations what he would be thinking after hearing the pregnancy news. "What's your first thought?" I asked. He was honest and started with, "Is she married?" Then he wanted to know, "Will she have another?" Both rather natural things to wonder, but each question clearly reveals an already established mind-set. And that's assuming that both thoughts occurred entirely unconsciously, and without any sort of malice.

An Aside: The Litmus Test

Periodically throughout this book, I will propose a litmus test for you to allow yourself to check your own unconscious and natural reactions. I ask you to think about this next example as a litmus test for measuring how we react to and think about people based on all of our underlying beliefs. This is a vehicle to help us see what we really believe—and how we unconsciously think.

Imagine again that you are a manager, and that this time a male employee (most likely a male) comes to tell you that—with a war raging in Iraq and troops being sent to Afghanistan—he has decided to join the U.S. Army National Guard or the British Territorial Army. What is your immediate reaction? Do you have a negative or positive feeling toward this person? The managerial challenges are similar to those surrounding the employee who announced she was pregnant. When is this person leaving? How long will he be gone? Who is going to do their work? Will he have to deploy again? What will this person be like when he returns from duty?

The mental litmus test allows you to check in on your own thinking. Ask yourself the following questions. Do I think the soldier is performing a higher duty or a noble action, and am I happy to figure out a way to accommodate him? Do I think the pregnant woman is really just a pain to manage, find that this is predictable, and think it would be easier if I didn't have women working for me? Maybe you see each situation similarly, or maybe you don't. Throughout this book, I will ask you to consider seriously whether you'd be okay if someone who looks like you did one thing but bothered if someone who is different from you did the exact same thing.

Language. In most globalized companies, English is typically the language of business. Yet even when people are all speaking English, unconscious thoughts can arise based on accents or expressions, especially if English is not a first language for everyone. A native English-speaking British colleague of mine once remarked to me about a Japanese colleague we both knew. "He is just getting smarter and smarter, as his English is getting better," said my colleague. I don't think he even realized what he was saying! Obviously, it was unconscious.

Although I cannot hear the difference between dialects spoken in England, British friends of mine say they can place a person by origin, class, and schooling as soon as they start to speak. I call this Verbal MapQuest. These friends say that after just a few words, they can narrow down the county, the public or private school from which the person graduated, and even their income level. It is amazing, but it can unconsciously affect how they think about the people around them. These judgments come fast and furiously, and the assumptions are made after only a few words.

We all do this to one degree or another. People with heavy southern accents aren't always taken as seriously in the United States; people pick out rural, urban, or regional accents all the time in any place on the planet as a way of subconsciously categorizing others and differentiating groups from one another. This is yet another piece of the puzzle that we call the Noah's ark of diversity. It is yet another reason why diversity is a stepping-stone but not the solution.

Positions, Titles, Seniority, Work Location within an Organization. There are dominant divisions, units, or jobs within an organization, and there are nondominant divisions, units, and positions. Whether we realize it or not, we *do* think differently about people in each category. Think about people who work in nondominant areas such as human resources, finance, technology, legal, and corporate services. This hierarchy is a subtle part of the ark. What do we really believe about them, and what assumptions are we truly making? Often what comes to mind is a person who is not as driven or willing to take risks, and someone who is important but not crucial to the organization. Dominant departments are easy to spot, as they are usually the revenue generators—groups that include the salespeople, the bankers, and the billing lawyers. They make the money. These dominant divisions and the people working in them tend to have more power, more prestige, and greater importance within an organization. Accordingly, we treat people differently and think about people differently depending on their title or position.

Hobbies. Differing hobbies can create an uneven playing field and create an organizational structure that is exclusionary, unfair, and can in turn create subtle advantages or disadvantages. Let's say that a manager loves golf, and that two of the people who work for him love golf. They chit chat about the sport and about their weekend games, and even go out to play golf together sometimes. Thanks to this, the two subordinates get a lot of access to the manager in a casual, unstructured way. These two people are also wisely working the system. They know that they have the manager's ear and may have the opportunity, in the middle of a golf game, to talk about what they are working on, how well it is going, or discuss their own career goals. Because the manager has a familiarity or friendship of sorts with these two, he will naturally be favorably inclined to the two employees who play golf with him and speak his language. Those employees who work for the manager but don't play golf or tennis or soccer won't get to that level of access. They won't have that comfortable chit chat, and won't have shared casual afternoons on the golf course or other shared off-hour hobbies with the manager.

Then, when the time comes for the manager to assign a project, share inside information, give out a promotion, or even a pay raise—he will be more inclined to turn to the people he knows best, who know him, and with whom he is most comfortable. There is a higher probability that he will be looking to give his golf buddies a raise, a promotion, or a new project before the others. And he isn't even being malicious or a bad manager. It is all quite natural and unconscious for the manager to entrust something new to the people on the team he has had an opportunity to get to know and trust. This is a classic way in which the meritocracy in a diverse organization can quickly erode.

Because of the prevalence of the golf culture in many companies, people often wonder if they need to learn to play the sport. No, you don't. Golf is simply another word for *access*. You do need to get access to the manager, which should be equal to the golfer's access. Managers who golf with some but not others need to be fully aware and fully conscious of how they can potentially create an unfair, unlevel playing field in Noah's ark. They need to be aware of the uneven access they are giving and the subtle advantage that is created. They have to find other ways to ensure the same access to the nongolfing employees, and the nongolfers need to find ways to obtain access to their manager.

Physical Appearance. We look at people, their hair, body type, weight, or dress, and quickly assess them fairly or unfairly based on these traits. Diversity consultant Kendall Wright uses an interesting exercise to prove this point. He asks people to write down what they think about when they think of a thin person, and then write down what they think about when they think of a fat person. If one is honest, he finds that we do have differing beliefs, assumptions, and unconscious reactions to body size. And, generally, we don't view heavier people favorably (although ironically, in some cultures, the opposite would be true).

In his book *Blink*, Malcolm Gladwell writes about the assumptions and perceptions around height. He indicates that in the United States, just 16 percent of men are 6 feet 2 inches or taller. When it comes to male Fortune 500 CEOs, there are 57 percent who are over 6 feet 2 inches; almost four times the number in the general population. I have read extensively on leadership and interviewed many world leaders. However, I have yet to see any research that correlates leadership capability and skeletal structure. Nevertheless, when we see tall men, we are likely to think: leader. We may change our minds if the tall man opens his mouth and speaks nonsense, but we've initially given him the benefit of the doubt. Shorter men are therefore at an automatic disadvantage. If you are shorter than average and walk into a room, few people will think leader unless proven otherwise. One has it until they lose it, while the other one doesn't have it until they prove it. One is a subtle advantage and one is a subtle disadvantage. One is easier, the other harder.

There are many other types of diversity in the ark, including habits or personality types such as those measured by the Myers-Briggs test or other personality test systems. You are focused and not easily distracted, but your employee is, from your perspective, easily distracted and difficult to pin down. They may see it as exploring options and staying open to new ideas. You are constantly frustrated and see no value in their way of approaching the world because it is not your way.

Perception in diversity can also be tricky because we will sometimes go looking for a trait that we *want* someone to have. We may purposefully search for something merely to confirm in our mind who that person is — or who we would like them to be. For example, if we see a tall man and think he is a leader, we invest in him leadership ability, assume that we can defer to him; and allow him to play that role — even if he hasn't earned it. That is likely to give the man confidence, which, ironically, is one of the predominant traits of leadership. It is a wonderful and virtuous cycle for the man who is given opportunities and chances that someone else might not have. It's not so easy for the shorter Hispanic male or the shorter female in whom we can't seem to bestow automatic confidence. Instead, these nondominant groups must expend an immense amount of time and effort proving themselves before we are willing to give them the label of leader.

I was intrigued to learn that when it comes to symphony orchestras, there is an old belief that women perform differently than men on musical instruments — not different and equal, mind you; rather, different and not quite as strong. If you believe someone plays less powerfully and you are watching him or her play, you might think to yourself, "I hear that sound less forcefully." Symphony orchestras around the world use blind auditions so that musicians are behind screens in order to prevent this belief from influencing a tryout. Some orchestras even found that they had to put carpeting on the audition hall floor, because a performer's shoes were a tell-tale sign of gender. In some auditions, if there is no carpeting, a female auditioner will take off her shoes and a man in shoes will walk beside her, so that the judges will assume they are listening to a male, therefore providing a subtle advantage to the performer. Blind auditions are not the perfect solution, but the number of women selected to play in orchestras has increased because of them.

Some literature has also found subtle beliefs about non-European musical performers. Chinese oboist Liang Wang experienced this first hand as a student at the Curtis Institute of Music in Philadelphia. A German composer once offered to show Wang how to play Brahms since he suspected he wouldn't know how, thanks to his nationality. "You don't have to be German to play Brahms," Wang told the *New York Times*. "I was very hurt. People think that way? It never occurred to me." Wang also described how, as a minority, he knew that he would have to be even more of a perfectionist than his Caucasian colleagues, and he knew he would have to endure more doubts about his mistakes. If he struggled with a

European composer, others might believe that perhaps it was because he was Asian. Or, as Wang sees it, perhaps it was simply because he was having an off day. Wang said he knew people saw his nationality and his Asian skin before they saw his raw talent and abilities. He's even been asked on more than one occasion, "Did you listen to classical music when you were growing up?" Of course, this master musician listened to classical music growing up—more than most Americans and Europeans. Today, Wang is the principal oboe player for the New York Philharmonic.

The academic field refers to this notion of "I know what I know because I know it" as confirmation bias. In the book *Mistakes Were Made (But Not by Me)*, authors Carol Tavris and Elliot Aronson call this perspective "implicit theory"—because people develop a theory about someone, but are unaware that they have done so. "The trouble is that once people develop an implicit theory, the confirmation bias kicks in and they stop seeing evidence that doesn't fit it." They then ignore or play down certain actions by the other, and exaggerate or are hypersensitive to certain other behaviors for the purpose of confirming their own internal theories. This can be especially dangerous in Noah's ark where there are so many differences and so many opportunities ripe for creating your own theory about what someone else is really like. It is easy to see things that fit your preconceived notions, hypotheses, or theories while dismissing other evidence that does not conform to what you have already decided. It's a trap. But the organization will not garner the true benefit of *hiring for difference*, realize the cognitive diversity of many ideas, or have a fair workplace as long as we continue to believe that we know what we know.

We must become truly aware of who is in the ark and what our unconscious thoughts tell us and lead us to do. Then we must act to overcome those subtle advantages or disadvantages that the diversity can create. The toughest piece of this is that we must stop making unconscious assumptions. That's not impossible, but it is difficult, and it will take time, practice, and a core realization that diversity itself is only the *first* step on the journey.

OBJECTIONS TO DIVERSITY

Knowing that this is a daunting task, it's no wonder that many people bristle at the thought of embracing diversity and moving beyond our differences. Some cringe at the mere mention of being asked to consider these issues. Often the dominant group individuals have the hardest time with these discussions. This isn't uncommon; it is in fact understandable, considering that most organizations haven't adequately implemented methods to allow diversity to succeed. I think it is important to acknowledge the ways in which this diversity discussion can rub people the wrong way. I go so far as to call these diversity issues myths, and can assure you that the fears about diversity's so-called evils are relatively unfounded.

- **Reverse discrimination.** Isn't it just unfair favoritism when the scale tips to the *other*? Some managers worry that they won't be able to hire the most qualified individuals, and would rather be asked to discriminate by selecting people based on their differences rather than what the hiring individual sees as the merits.

- **Defies the meritocracy of the organization**. If we are using a different yardstick to measure qualifications for the diverse candidates, aren't we just lowering the standards of our organization—all to accommodate the minorities?

- **Coddling the diverse individuals**. Those in the dominant group often fear that they will have to be politically correct, avoid giving critical feedback, and treat the diverse employees more gingerly. This includes a fear of walking on eggshells and having to accept compromised performance.

- **Lack of evidence**. Many are skeptical that diversity is a tool for success, because they haven't read business cases that outline empirical evidence to support these claims.

- **Rocking the boat**. Change is admittedly hard; adding new dynamics to a group may shift power and could even change the familiar inner circles. It is unnerving for many in those power groups to think that they would have to share the limelight, the boardroom, or the credit they are used to receiving.

- **It's all about the law.** Some see the need to embrace diversity as merely a mandate that is being forced upon them by the law or by the desire to present a positive image to the public. They see the laws governing discrimination as a mere obstacle and resent Equal Employment Opportunity Commission (EEOC)-type regulations or perceived quotas.

- **Don't blame me.** Individuals in the nondominant, diverse groups worry that they will be seen as taking advantage of the system or having only gotten a promotion because of their race, religion, or difference and not on their merits. This leaves some of the diverse crowd wishing the whole subject would simply go away so that they won't have to wonder if their colleagues are resentful or skeptical of their success.

These objections to diversity are truly objections to the challenges buried in having a diverse workplace. If we agree that our workplaces *are* going to be diverse, then we need to change the structures, raise awareness, level the playing fields, and actually demonstrate to ourselves how much more successful, productive, and globally competitive we can be by embracing these differences rather than fighting them and the necessary changes. In truth, it is rare in this day and age for a company to have a meritocracy already in place. Most have the pieces of diversity in place—the animals on the ark—but haven't achieved a place where "like" and "not like" are treated the same. There is always someone who is taller, went to the right school, played the popular sport, and has a subtle advantage. There are others, because of their difference from the dominant group, who are subtly disadvantaged. We are not talking about blatant inequities or discrimination in most of today's professional world (although this still does occur). We are talking about unconscious beliefs, preferences, values, thoughts, and actions. Those are what erode the promise of diversity, and why we need to get beyond diversity. We must understand the diversity dynamic—the part that the unconscious plays—so that we can be aware and overcome the ones that erode fairness in an organization. Only then can we capitalize on differences and find ways to succeed because of diversity rather than in the face of it. In that way, we will build stronger, truer meritocracies capable of extraordinary results.

Now for the tools and awareness that will assist in getting us there.

Chapter 2

The Elephant and the Mouse

In every power structure on Earth, there are elephants and there are mice. The basic idea is that if you are the elephant in the room, what do you need to know about the mouse? Not much, for you are mighty, tall, and powerful, and have little use for the tiny jungle creatures. If you are the mouse in the room, what do you need to know about the elephant? Everything. You could be crushed or obliterated if you don't understand the elephant's habits, movements, and preferences.

The elephant knows almost nothing about the mouse, while the mouse survives by knowing everything about the other. Herein lies the dynamic between the dominant and nondominant groups in the workplace. Nondominant groups develop certain skill sets, including vigilance, attentiveness, and adaptability. In business, for example, Microsoft is an elephant and Mozilla is a mouse.

31

In politics, the United States is the elephant; Hong Kong is a mouse. In American society, generally white men are elephants, while women and minorities are mice.

We cannot escape the fact that some groups have more power than others. This power may come from sheer numbers, who historically has had more power, or pre-conceived ideas about the proper roles of individuals in a given culture. All of these will affect who naturally has a dominant place in the power structure and who does not. It also affects what we know about others, how much we know about what other's lives are like, and what others experience. It reflects the skill sets we develop as we grow up, and how culture, society, and family influence us.

I am always amazed by how much people in other countries know about the United States. It isn't uncommon for a citizen of Sweden to know about the governor of California; yet not many U.S. citizens are aware of who the prime minister of Sweden is. Think about how knowledgeable the world was about the recent election of Barack Obama; now think how little the average American knows about Kenya, Obama's father's birthplace.

The parable of the elephant and the mouse illustrates how people operate in the world. The dominant group person assumes that the world operates for everyone in the way it operates for them. They feel a strong sense of control over their environment, and feel entitled to go the way they want. The nondominant, mouse-like individual learns to be vigilant and read people carefully. "A white man with a PhD may know little about a black man's life," says megachurch Bishop T. D. Jakes. "But a black man with a GED knows almost everything about how white men live." Similarly, former president of Ireland Mary Robinson commented to me that the Irish know much more about the English than the English ever know about the Irish.

When asked about the elephant and mouse theory, moderator and managing editor of PBS's *Washington Week* and senior correspondent for *The NewsHour with Jim Lehrer*, Gwen Ifill, related the following incident—which illustrates the complexity that emanates from racial disparities between dominant and nondominant groups.

I had a conversation with a member of Congress a few days ago who looked me in the eye, and with a completely straight face, making his argument against the voting rights act, told me there is no more racism in America where he travels, and so he doesn't know why it is needed. Then he told me off camera, with great pride, about how he derailed the renewal of the voting rights act at the Republican Caucus meeting. And he told me proudly how a colleague walked up to him afterwards and told him, "That was a lynching in there." Now, this member of Congress said this to me smiling.... Because he doesn't believe racism exists, it didn't occur to him on any level that he was insulting me. But he can only see what he said as an insult if he were to give up his assumption that racism doesn't exist. And he could only think that racism doesn't exist if he believes that the way he lives his life is the norm.

Renowned U.S. economist Laura Tyson described her journey when she became dean of the London Business School. She observed the following:

> I have power in principle, but actually I was foreign to the institution. The institution had all sorts of rules and behavior and people who had networks. How do you figure out who these people are and what their tasks and rules of behavior are? Who talks to whom? Who are they? You have to figure all that out. You have to develop the skill to watch. Which is not what people recruit leaders for. They don't say this person is a good watcher . . . I had to watch them as much as they watched me. They had the knowledge. I had to figure it out.

The best leaders in this new global environment—be it corporate or political—need the skill sets that both the elephant and the mouse possess. Leaders in diverse organizations must realize that their dominance might not reflect the situation for others in the organization. In other words, the leader who has the most positive attributes, culled from the elephant and the mouse, will triumph.

The dominant elephant feels entitled to speak, knows without question what it wants, doesn't watch all that much, and isn't terribly concerned about what the mouse is up to. On the other hand, the mouse, out of necessity, has developed strong emotional intelligence. Imagine that the elephant occasionally likes to play poker with the mouse. How well do you think the elephant *reads* the mouse? Not well, I can assure you. But there is danger in abusing your elephant power and ignoring the mice in your organization, warns Pepper Schwartz, a professor of sociology at the University of Washington in Seattle. "If you are an elephant, you might not notice that the mice population has grown. You get a Gulliver's Travels kind of approach. Or, if you want to think of it in human terms—you get a revolution." Schwartz points out that if ignored or abused long enough, mice will rise up and exert their own form of power. "The classic case is the secretary who sees all the documents come through, while she notices that the boss is taking his mistress on business trips—and holds onto that information. She may be in a small position, but she's not stupid and she keeps that for a rainy day if she needs it." Schwartz adds, "A lot of elephants have been brought down by mice. If you don't recognize who the mice are, what they need, and respect their space—they are going to get you."

Ask female poker players what their playing strengths are, and many will tell you that they are skilled at reading body language. In a *Time* magazine article about why women are so successful at playing poker, one woman said, "From the time we're teens, we wonder, 'Will he call? What's he thinking?' Women have their intuition more honed." That said, male poker players do often win greater sums of money because of their willingness to take greater risks (an elephantine characteristic), while women have shrewder instincts about when not to gamble their sums. Imagine how successful you could be at poker if you had the shrewd instincts of the mouse and took the risks of the elephant.

The women may have developed a scarcity mentality, something Muhammad Yunus of the Grameen Bank (established to help the poor) has experienced when making microloans to women. "They don't go from one cow to a 100 cow loan as men would with the higher risk that entails; they go from one cow to five cows. The female instincts are uniquely honed because they are more likely to *need* to understand the behaviors of the dominant power group." In Chapter 4, I'll discuss further how important it is for today's business leaders to possess the tools of both the elephant and the mouse. It takes both sets of these skills to be successful in a diverse and globalized twenty-first-century organization.

I have always been intrigued by where the concept of *women's intuition* comes from, and whether there is evidence to support this notion. President Robinson noted that women are often more likely to observe, have better listening skills, include others not normally included, have more emotional intelligence, be less hierarchical, and develop more intuitive observations. However, she also told me that she felt that while traditionally these were considered female traits, she believes they are traits acquired by most groups or individuals who have been out of power historically. Those who have not been in power will develop those intuitive skills in the interest of survival.

For example, women typically get more practice understanding and processing emotions, and are even encouraged to do so from an early age. In turn, they focus in on the signs that others exhibit through verbal or nonverbal means to express their feelings. They can sense and perceive through practice how other people in a room are feeling, receiving information, or reacting. Dr. Ashley Montagu—revered for his work on race and gender's relationship to politics and society—suggests that women have actually honed more perceptual speed in picking up clues, because society has urged them to do so, and that this is something taught and encouraged beginning at a very young age.

Cherie Blair QC, barrister, wife of the former British Prime Minister Tony Blair, says she's acutely aware of how much women are attuned to people around them, and how they study behaviors and actions out of a need to fit in and ultimately succeed. Blair noticed this when she went to a play at the Globe Theatre in London, which produces Shakespeare's plays as they would have been performed originally. Typically, the women are played by men, but

one performance—*The Taming of the Shrew*—included
a cast entirely of women. She attended the performance
with her husband and noticed that the women were playing the male roles more convincingly than the men played
the women's roles in previous performances. "There is
always something slightly unconvincing about men who
play the women," she said. "The girl who played Petruchio
[the lead male]; I just thought she was the most fantasti-
cally convincing man. I think the reason she was such a
convincing man is that women have to observe the men
the whole time, so therefore when it came to playing a
man, she knew what to do. When the male actors play the
women, they play the women as they *think* women are."

The ways in which men and women observe the world
do have an influence over workplace, politics, and society. "As more women come into public leadership, there
will be a blurring of styles," says Janet Napolitano, Secretary of Homeland Security and former Arizona governor.
When Napolitano was elected Arizona's Attorney General in 1999, she quickly experienced what it was like to
be the mouse. "In my first week I was with all men, and
they used acronyms and referenced cases I hadn't been
familiar with," she recalled to me. "At first I felt mouse-
like, observing and listening and learning the ways. And
then it didn't take long to feel elephant-like." Being from
Arizona, Napolitano was aware of the assumptions and
stereotypes she and her fellow Arizonans faced from the
rest of the country. There were things that people assumed

or had once learned and were stuck with. "Arizona has lots of stereotypes," says Napolitano. "Like it is old, slow, and has lots of cactus. It is one of the fastest growing and youngest states. The population of Denmark is less than Arizona."

I believe that learned behaviors and assumptions can be seen in other nondominant groups whose success and survival depend on knowing the dominant group's habits and ways of being. Those with less power are forced into this role. A similar dynamic existed in the relationship between the colonizer and the colonized; the master and slave; the served and the servant; or really, any dominant and nondominant group. Those who are in power are less likely to know the details about those who are not in power. The powerless, in fact, are far more likely to be aware of the powerful through listening, observing, and honing their antennae.

"If there is asymmetrical power, power goes to the less dependent entity," says Joseph Nye, Jr., Harvard Kennedy School of Government professor and author of *Soft Power: The Means to Success in World Politics*. "The elephant is inattentive to the mouse, and the mouse has to learn agile and adaptive skills." Nye applies similar thinking to men and women. "You could say that women are more used to using soft power, and men more used to using hard power. Successful leaders use 'smart power'—a combination of the two. One might says, 'Let's fight.' The other might say, 'Let's talk.' "

I look at the parable of the elephant and the mouse as a leadership and diversity paradigm—because with diversity comes asymmetrical power. Organizations will have people who are culturally dominant as members, and if diverse, will have employees who are culturally nondominant in some way. How each exists in the world is shaped by each one's juxtaposed position.

Again, it comes down to what the elephant ends up knowing about the mouse's experience, what the mouse ends up knowing about the elephant's, and what skills were honed by the *not watching* and the *watching*. The mouse will have to carefully sharpen his observational and listening skills. Does the flit of the elephant's tail mean he is moving backward? What about a flapping ear? Is the elephant signaling that he is hungry? The mouse will become finely tuned to the elephant because a sudden backward movement, for example, could seriously impact the little mouse. The elephant, on the other hand, has less of a need to know the habits of the mouse. The elephant moves where it wants, speaks its voice loudly, feels entitlement to ask for what it wants, and is less concerned about what the mouse is doing or thinking. It moves forthrightly and without hesitating or constantly monitoring the mouse's movements. But as political consultant and Harvard professor David Gergen points out, "The really good leaders are the ones that do notice."

Think about how much people will know about the CEO of an organization where they are working. If she asks for coffee in the morning without first greeting her assistant, the assistant can discern that the CEO is harried and grouchy, and will adjust to accommodate. The movie *The Devil Wears Prada* offers a classic example of a boss whose needs, habits, and desires are the total focus and anticipation of her assistants. Miranda Priestly, played by Meryl Streep, is the editor-in-chief of a high profile magazine, who can't be bothered to remember her assistant's name. Instead, she barks orders to her assistant, who is supposed to anticipate her boss's every need and even answer to whichever name she is called—or else worry about being fired.

COMBINING FORCES

My basic thesis surrounding the elephant and the mouse is that the best leaders in diverse organizations need to develop a skill set that incorporates both animals and both ways of being in the world. It is the only way to navigate in diverse groups where not everyone is experiencing the same thing. It's crucial that a successful person have the elephant's confidence to speak in his own voice without hesitation; to move toward where she or he wants to go without ever worrying or being paralyzed by the possibility that others will be unhappy if they ask for what they want. The sense of entitlement that is felt by being large and in power can be a beneficial trait to possess.

Simultaneously, leaders must combine the elephant-like traits with the mouse's intuitively honed ability to read people, understand their behaviors, and multitask (the mouse can eat and be aware of the elephant's movements at the same time). You might say the mouse has what we humans know as emotional intelligence. The best leaders and most successful people combine the strongest elements of each of these creatures. Again, I think of the professional poker player. If you could combine the skills of the women who can read the male card players with the slightly greater risk-taking tendencies and the willingness to bet more money—you'd end up with one very successful card player.

Ultimately, it is about what happens in the dynamics of diverse organizations. We have to get beyond diversity and realize that there is an additional dimension at play between dominant and nondominant individuals or groups. "So many of these traits have to do with the position of subordination, rather than intricate characteristics of gender or races or sexes," says Christine Di Stefano, associate professor of political science and adjunct professor of women's studies at the University of Washington, who refers to this as a social constructionist view. Basically, this means you could look at the dominant elephant and subordinate mouse through a variety of lenses—from class, education level, profession, or where in the country someone lives. "You can do a lot with the strengths of perspectives and orientations that are garnered from the subordinate positions; but you don't want to overdo it, because there are liabilities," says Di Stefano. "Some of those liabilities include adopting the identity of the victim." It is important to see that within the mouse's framework, there are shortcomings that would be counterintuitive for managers to adopt. It is productive to seek out the strongest traits but not to arbitrarily adopt the subordinate group's fate, perspectives, or weaknesses.

On occasion, these subordinate groups become populated with enough similar people—for example, two women in a company become 25—that the dominant group is forced to take this other perspective seriously. It is no longer a choice, and they begin to notice. "When you get enough mice together in an organization or leadership capacity, they can begin to change the dynamics of leadership," says Di Stefano. When this happens, it's possible that the dominant group will "accede to a different way of doing business."

All of this means that the dominant group may in fact be capable of absorbing some of the traits of the nondominant group. These traits are not inherent to a particular race, size, language, nationality, or gender group, but rather learned and accepted traits of the nondominant culture. Implicit in this acknowledgment is that it *is* in fact possible for the dominant group to become flexible, or develop new ways of acting or thinking. In a diverse organization, listening and observing are crucial. Therefore it is important, if not imperative, that the mouse adapt and adopt some of those elephant-like traits, and that the elephant do the same with regard to the strengths of the mouse.

Take former United States Representative Heather Wilson of New Mexico—a strong leader with mouse-like intuition and perspective, and elephantesque qualities—who explains that at its core, leadership is about communicating. "If you can't communicate, you can't lead," explains Wilson, a Republican who served the first United States congressional district from 1998 to 2008. An impressively accomplished woman, graduate of the Air Force Academy and Rhodes Scholar, Wilson is aware of her unusual position in society. In order to remain in touch with the people who may feel subordinate to her, Wilson routinely talks about her children, and refers to them in an effort to let people know that they may have something in common. Parents raising difficult teenagers can often relate to one another. Wilson explains, "I have one of the most diverse congressional districts in the country [United States]; socio-economically [and] ethnically. And part of being a good public leader is having people comfortable with you."

Wilson is conscious of how she achieves this. "Some of [it is] nonverbal; some of it is [done] by consciously being where people don't expect you to be." Once, while talking to a group of African Americans, Wilson made sure to tell a story that would illustrate that she understood what it was like to be a part of the nondominant minority.

She told about having arrived at the Air Force Academy as one of few women, feeling small and out of place. It earned her respect with a group of people who might have otherwise thought that she—a well-educated and accomplished white woman—couldn't relate to their own painful obstacles.

"Too many leaders try to build groups [with members] that look like themselves," says Wilson. This is the inherent problem with the company manager always playing golf with the golfing subordinates. Even though the manager might not consciously be excluding other nongolfing candidates for an upcoming promotion, he will be more inclined to go for the employees who think, look, and act like him.

There is also the issue of entitlement. As Wilson also points out, an individual in a dominant group can assume his or her role or responsibility with ease. There is a presumed competence with those in the dominant group and a questioned competence surrounding those in the nondominant group. The elephant is assumed to be a strong, mighty animal. Any strength that the mouse might have must be well-proven, and is never initially assumed. Likewise, in a company where golfing men are dominant, other similarly inclined men will be at an advantage. People will assume that they, too, must be competent, good leaders worthy of a raise, a promotion, or of just being given a chance. Therefore, a shy minority who has never picked up a golf club will have to work additionally hard to prove his or her worth, reliability, and intelligence. This is why diversity done unconsciously simply does not work.

POINT OF VIEW

An important piece of the elephant and mouse parable is point of view. Each one of these animals sees the same world, jungle, or threats from a different perspective and has a different outlook. HSBC Bank captures the diversity of viewpoints brilliantly with their somewhat ironic ad campaign. In one ad, there are two photos—one of a dog, and the other of a cat. Next to those photos is an identical pair of photos with the same dog and cat. Over the first dog is the word "love" and over the first cat is the word "loathe." But over the second dog, which is the same exact animal, is the word "loathe," and over that same long-haired cat is "love." The idea, of course—depending on the audience's viewpoint—is that each animal is seen in an entirely different way. If you're a feline lover, the cat will indeed evoke warm and fuzzy feelings, but if you can't stand the creatures, then you'll relate better with the overlaid word "loathe." The company offers similar ads that depict an antique water wheel alongside a mass of graffiti and the words "art" as well as "rubbish." Of course, we're getting into personal style, preference, and opinion, as one person's idea of art is another person's idea of utter garbage. The same situation or object can elicit very different responses or reactions.

The same thing must occur in diverse organizations. One person sees the strength in their own particular way of doing things, and would consider another's methods to be weak, simply because it isn't their way.

At Goldman Sachs, there is a keen awareness of the dynamics of diversity, power, and point of view. In 2008, the bank invested $100 million in a new program called *10,000 Women*, to identify, educate, and mentor women in developing countries and the United States to become entrepreneurs. Goldman Sachs chairman Lloyd Blankfein was clear in starting the program—he knew that these women, if properly educated and mentored, had the potential to become highly productive in their communities. He was also aware that these women had been members of the less powerful, nondominant groups in their societies and cultures. They needed the opportunities that the dominant group—in this case, men in business—had received *naturally* in their communities.

When we work in a world that is as diverse as Noah's ark, we must become consciously aware that *my* point of view or *my* set of experiences and opportunities are not the same as *yours*. That is what makes diversity both so valuable and so challenging. Just because your comments haven't repeatedly been ignored in a meeting thanks to who you are, does not mean that it isn't happening to someone else. How you are evaluated may be very different than how your colleague is evaluated because of our own point of view. But just having an awareness of this reality will get you halfway to succeeding in this post-diversity environment. The journey continues from there.

Chapter 3

Tell Your Grandma to Go Home

Grandma always has a lesson or two to share; my grand-mother certainly did. Even for those of us without an actual grandmother to pass along wisdom and quirky expressions, society has provided us with a grandma of sorts. We've all inherited our unconscious beliefs about the world through a variety of channels—be it from parents, friends at school, teachers, neighborhood attitudes, or the television. These beliefs include our own experiences, the media, the myths and legends we learn as children, our belief system and religious instruction. All of these channels unconsciously provide us with a point of view that in turn informs our perspective of others and ourselves. I call these channels "Grandma." It is shorthand for the different ways we learn about ourselves and others, and even though we are all professional adults as we enter the workplace, we bring Grandma with us. She sits next to us in meetings, performance reviews, interviews, conference calls, and at any other time we are at work.

For example, in the United States, Grandma customarily taught men that "The squeaky wheel gets the grease," implying that the person who complains the loudest often receives the most attention. Or that if you speak up in class, at work, or at a party you will get noticed—and even rewarded. However, in Japan it's said that, "The nail that sticks out gets hit on the head." The squeaky wheel is a far cry from the lesson taught by the Chinese Grandma, who says, "The loudest duck gets shot." Being outspoken in these cultures is discouraged; it is 180 degrees opposite the squeaky wheel. Asian nationalities contend that the one who speaks up is punished, not rewarded. This couldn't be more different from what the American in your workplace has learned from Grandma.

What do these aphorisms tell us about how individualism, ambition, and conformity are viewed from the perspective of these different cultures? There is that familiar lesson in humility from Grandma—often told specifically to girls—that "If you can't say anything nice, don't say anything at all." How does this saying shape the recipient of the message? How does it translate in a corporate culture when we bring our unconscious lessons from Grandma into the workplace? How does it influence how we act and react? Of course, for women the 'nice' message, like the Asian messages, is the complete opposite of the squeaky wheel message.

All of these cultural aphorisms—handed down from generation to generation, and distilled from "Grandma's Lessons of Life"—are closely adhered to by the respective cultures. It's not surprising that many American workers—from the dominant white male culture in particular—understand and embrace the squeaky wheel metaphor. But it's unlikely that the American manager would perceive his Japanese employee's reticence to speak up at a strategic planning meeting as a direct consequence of that employee's cultural template of deference. It's more likely that the employee would be considered not assertive enough or lacking ideas. We forget that we are taught to carry ourselves, share opinions, and offer praise differently. We forget that even though we are all adults, we still bring Grandma to work with us each day.

Here is how diversity *doesn't* work: if a manager in a traditional corporate setting is conducting a meeting and they have a Wheel, a Nail, a Duck, and a Nice as employees sitting around the meeting table—chances are the Wheel is attracting all of the attention by doing all of the talking. The other three are quietly engaged in the task at hand, but they do not venture into the verbal fray. It's not because they lack excellent ideas—they probably have many—but Grandma told them not to speak up, so they don't. The manager unconsciously listens to all of the Wheel's good ideas, does not hear from the others, passes judgment that no one else has anything to contribute, and ultimately promotes the Wheel for all of his or her good ideas. The organization loses out on the cognitive diversity that the Nail, the Duck, and the Nice bring to the table. So, after all that careful hiring of diverse groups, all the committees, networks and corporate statements, all you get are the Wheels talking and everyone else listening. You haven't achieved the real, cognitive diversity that we are seeking in a company. You can never achieve the type of success necessary to compete in a global business environment if only the Wheels are being heard. Worse, the Nails, Ducks, and the Nice are likely to be unfairly evaluated and ultimately subtly disadvantaged. In this scenario, their playing field is not level. Those who have the subtle disadvantage may get so frustrated that they end up leaving, so in the end, our diversity drove our diversity away.

This dynamic is experienced repeatedly during the ubiquitous global conference call. The American manager says into the speaker, "Anyone have anything to say?" and there is silence (or clicking of the computer keys). No one speaks up. What happened to the cognitive diversity we were looking for? It is gone because only the Wheels are speaking up.

NECESSARY BUT NOT SUFFICIENT

Many major businesses have taken a serious and informed strategy for incorporating diversity into their workplace. Most offer a strong business case for having a workforce that is diverse—for example, the war for talent; trying to recruit and retain the best people; the need to better reflect an organization's clients; the higher profitability; the global nature of the firm; the legal scrutiny and laws now prevalent in many countries. These companies have put the building blocks in place, so what you see are the trainings, the senior-level rhetoric and commitment, the various diversity-related committees, and the networks for women, blacks, Asians or Hispanics, or gays and lesbians.

I don't believe that these foundational efforts will actually change cultures. While I am not suggesting that we get rid of these building blocks, I don't think that they will ever level the playing field or create true meritocracies for everyone who works within a corporation. They are not sufficient. Why? Because we all take our unconscious selves to the workplace—whether we mean to or not. Again, we bring our beliefs, perceptions, understandings, misunderstandings, and our archetypes of who we think people are. We incorporate these impressions instinctively as we think, speak, and even act in ways that we've deemed natural. By doing so, we guarantee that the playing field will remain unbalanced, and that the organization of which we are a part will never truly get the benefit of its diversity, or function at its highest level.

People tend to believe that their colleagues within an organization are professional and approach the world in a common way. After all, we all work for the same company.

In fact, people will act and think in the same natural way that they would in a bar socializing. We may choose to use different words at work, but our general approach to a group of people at work and in a social situation are largely the same. Whether we're at a business meeting or a birthday party, we form opinions, express ourselves, and size up those around us. There are the elephants and the mice. Thanks to Grandma, we bring our feelings of chemistry, preferences, archetypes, and images about others to our jobs; ultimately, we are all less professional and logical than we think we are. We bring what all the societal forces taught us into our professional settings. *We each have our own narrative, our own "story" about who we are and who others are. We react to others and others react to us through that narrative, whether our story is true or not.* Add to all of this the dynamic of the elephant and the mouse and the many types of diversities in the ark, and you can see how difficult it is to create a fair workplace. It's also easy to see why we often do not reap the true value of our differences.

PRECONCEIVED NOTIONS HAVE ROOTS

When it comes to the professional world, the proverbs and lessons that every culture's Grandma taught us result in very distinct ways of doing business—none of which are necessarily the right way or even the better way. If you were to sit down at a business meeting in Guangzhou or Hokkaido or Hanoi, the atmosphere would be strangely different from the loud, combative financial meetings you often find on Wall Street. By taking the time to understand the viewpoints through which others see the world and learn more tools, company executives, managers, and employees can understand how better to work with them and ultimately become more effective. By being conscious about our own Grandma and those of others, we can do what is essential to ensure that our workplace is fair as well as diverse.

So, how exactly do we end up with these unconscious and natural beliefs, assumptions, perceptions, and archetypes? Harvard social psychologist Mahzarin Banaji has long studied the ways in which irreplaceable notions are ingrained in the human brain. She has been testing people's natural reactions for years, and her findings have shown that there are certain unconscious reactions that the brain gives off to people who are not like you. In other words, perception is ingrained—no matter who you are. She has also found that these preferences begin forming at the age of six. That's when her studies reveal that children will choose to be with other children who look similar, rather than with children who appear differently. As we age, certain faces are naturally associated with more positive or negative reactions. Asians may become more appealing on gut reaction, while African Americans may become less so. Even though consciously we might entirely reject these findings, Banaji's work reveals that at times, our brains are working against our best intentions.

Few would disagree that our ideas about the world begin with early childhood and continue, almost uninterrupted, throughout our entire lives. Let's look at five of the major unconscious forces to understand better the origin of our beliefs and preconceived ideas, as well as to get a handle on how we can wrestle these ideas to the ground.

Our unconscious thinking originates with:

1. **Our parents**. The parental units put a lot of material into our heads—both overtly and covertly. After all, we heard messages from them before we did from almost anyone else. They fed their ideas to us from an early age. From them, we gather who is good and who is bad, something they often communicate quite unconsciously through subtle behaviors or comments. They also lay out their expectations for us based on our gender. Girls should do one thing, or act a certain way; boys should act another way, and are expected to behave differently. We watch our parents, looking for a signal—usually unbeknownst to us—about how we should react to situations and people. We wait to see how they react to hearing that their child is gay or lesbian. We hear them explain nationalities, skin color, and their own ideas about differences. Even if we ultimately reject some of it, we absorb it all. The parental influence is overwhelmingly powerful. Just ask any therapist.

2. **Our experiences**. Every day we learn something from our experiences, and we extrapolate from the world around us based on what we see, learn, and do. If you walk down the hallway of a corporation past the lineup of photographs of the previous CEOs, you're likely to see a wall of older white males in American corporations, or older Japanese men in Japan. That's what sticks in our minds about what is valued at most companies and what is valued in Noah's ark. Most major institutions— government departments, universities, and companies— have walls of photos like these that provide a constant reminder about who is typically on top and who is dominant.

Iceland's Vigdis Finnbogadottir was the first and the longest sitting woman president in the world (1980–1996). When I spoke with her, she told me that after about eight years in office, she started to notice that children under the age of eight often thought that *only* a woman could be president. President Vigdis had many boys ask her if the president of Iceland could be a male. Because the boys had only ever known a woman to be president, they didn't understand that they could possibly be president of their country some day. This is one way we learn how the world works, especially when we are young and impressionable—understanding the future of the world to be as we see it at that moment. We quickly come to believe that our experiences and our observations represent not only *how* the world works but also how it *should* work.

I call this the power of the mirror. We know what we can be by what we see.

A good friend of mine and father of a four-year-old described an experience he had with his young daughter at a large toy store. He told his daughter that she could pick out a toy, within reason. She said she wanted an action, GI Joe-type doll. As she started to reach for the toy, a woman clerk walked by and said to her, "Oh, you don't want that; that's a boy's toy." My friend was apoplectic and told his daughter she could have the toy. The little girl turned to him and said to her father, "I don't want this. It's a boy's toy."

This can happen early, and it can happen often. In many countries, we dress little girls in pink and we dress little boys in blue (or other distinguisher). Try dressing them in yellow and, of course, the first question will be, is it a boy or a girl?

3. **Our peers**. Peers, perhaps more so than teachers, are a strong influence — especially when we are young. We listen, watch, and develop our beliefs based upon what our peers do or tell us. Names get called, people get humiliated, some are allowed into the "in" crowd, and others get the message that they are lacking something and therefore are relegated to the "out" group.

Through one of its studies, the American Council on Education looked at gender expectations in young children. A group of 11-year-old girls were asked, "What would it be like if you came back tomorrow as a boy?" The girls responded that they would climb trees, get dirty, and play late. A group of 11-year-old boys were similarly asked, "What would happen if you came back tomorrow as a girl?" The boys' reactions? Nearly suicidal. Some said that they would jump off a bridge, wouldn't wake up the next day in hopes of ignoring the reality, or wouldn't go out of the house. The boys reacted with mortification and horror at the thought of having to live life as a girl.

The influence of nature versus nurture often comes up when discussing how gender affects young children, and how they make their way in the world. The American Council on Education research seems to show that something happened between birth and 11 years of age that led the girls to be okay with the idea of changing genders, and the boys to be suicidal at the mere thought of it. Some of this negativity around being a girl comes from peer behavior, labeling, and taunting. However, these attitudes aren't displayed only by young people. Once while exercising at my gym, I overheard a personal trainer telling one of his male clients, "You're lifting weights like a girl." We all understand that this is just about the *last* thing a man wants to be told.

It isn't uncommon for teens to resort to all-out cruelty toward their gay or lesbian peers. In 2008, a gay eighth grader died after being shot by a classmate in his California school. Taunts are rampant in high schools, and slurs are commonly used to describe anyone who is different. There is, of course, the use of faggot or dyke; some still even use the N word. Others resort to referring to a Muslim as Osama Bin Laden to cast an insult. Although well embedded in our minds, most of us consciously reject these epithets. It's hard not to attach labels, even ones we wouldn't say out loud, to people we see every day. Then we arrive in the corporate Noah's ark with all of our own historical baggage.

4. **Religion and culture**. These are major forces telling us who we and others are, who is right, and who is wrong. There are the believers and the nonbelievers, the infidels, and the "other." Most of us want to believe that religion and culture are vehicles for peace and understanding; but they can be just as much a vehicle for providing unconscious *natural* thoughts about who is around us, working next to us, or living in our neighborhoods. Our various houses of worship teach us that we are right and others are wrong or are sinners for not sharing our beliefs. It is difficult to put aside those unconscious thoughts when we sit in a business meeting or when our children play together in the back yard.

5. **Myths, fairy tales, fables, and the media**. Those centuries-old tales that many of us remember with fondness are not just innocent bedtime stories. Many fairy tales and fables instead offer up extreme and long-lasting archetypes and values that have been passed down from generation to generation. They shape who we are, and are constantly transmitted and carried—often unknowingly—by the media. Transmitted subliminally,

many contain strong and enduring assumptions about women's roles, men's importance, and how society should be.

For example, the hero's journey is a classic story that our society seems to love—and one that we often see portrayed in the media. As a fairy tale or fable, this is the story about the young man who must go out into the world to slay the dragon, defeat the enemy, and find the Holy Grail. He may fail at first, and thus strengthen the enemy. But our archetype hero always comes back, finds the strength to complete his mission, and ultimately is victorious. The hero then returns to his kingdom or tribe to claim his reward, which may be the keys to the kingdom, some other riches, and usually the hand of the fair maiden.

Hollywood and Bollywood rely heavily on this story line—from *Spiderman* and *Superman* to the many *Rocky* movies with Sylvester Stallone. Many of Bruce Willis's films follow this structure; in particular, the various *Die Hard* movies. We see the same appeal in *Star Wars*, *Star Trek*, *Gladiator*, *300*, *The Matrix*, *Shrek*, and the James Bond, Indiana Jones, Western cowboy, and even Harry Potter movies. The hero's journey is not necessarily a bad myth for leadership; after all, it focuses on passion, determination, unblinking dedication, overcoming great odds, and the vision to be successful. These are all traits we encourage in our leaders. It is a positive myth in many ways. However, the problem is that almost without exception, the hero is male and is often known as "The White Knight" (an unconscious nod to both gender and skin color).

Another popular type of fable relies on the "rescue" or "rescue me" construct. This is best illustrated with the classic story of *Cinderella*, who is known for cleaning the fireplace, combating the evil stepmother and stepsisters, and talking to mice. When the poor girl finally gets to go to the ball, she meets the Prince who falls in love with her, finds her lost shoe, and swoops in to rescue Cinderella from her terrible life. There are hundreds of versions of *Cinderella* throughout the world's storytelling, and it remains a favorite of young girls everywhere. The first known version is found in a ninth-century Chinese story in which a magical fish, rather than a fairy godmother, helps the heroine, Yeh-shen, and the king uses a golden slipper to identify and rescue this otherwise helpless girl.

Sleeping Beauty, another well-known fairy tale, is the epitome of the "rescue me" myth. The heroine, with her long dark hair and angelic face, is facing a terrible destiny as she lies unconscious on a table. She is breathing, but has no other life to her; that is, until the Prince comes along and kisses her, at which point she awakens (metaphor) and is brought to life. Only thanks to the man can she be part of the world again. These rescue myths are not good myths for leadership. These individuals did not rely on their own capabilities, but rather on the strength of others. And who is this rescued person most often found in these tales? Invariably, a female. (I have yet to figure out *Snow White and the Seven Dwarfs*—she just seems like a woman multitasking with seven little men.)

These prevalent characters—dancing on the pages of our storybooks or across our TV screens—all contain elements that encourage and teach us how to view the world. We start with *Cinderella* and *Superman,* and end up carrying our *knowledge* of the way the world works—of who rescues and who needs to be rescued—right into the workplace. We think we are professional and acting in conscious ways, but these are the images and messages—the Grandmas—that we haul around with us every day. In a diverse organization, we are sure to have many different Grandmas around the table. We assume our professionalism and yet Grandma comes to work and sits next to us every day, whispering in our ear.

Chapter 4

What's Easy for You Is Hard for Me and How to Navigate the Differences

Consider how you might handle the following situation if you were a company manager overseeing a very skilled and productive employee: this employee's manager is not noticing the extent of his hard work. The manager doesn't think to mention the employee, and the executives above the manager know nothing about the employee's especially strong performance. What do you make of this situation? Most of the managers I work with react similarly after hearing this scenario. They tend to say that the employee should "just speak up," tell their manager about what they've been doing, and ask that he or she get them in front of the more senior team. This is an obvious solution for these managers, because they would do just that.

But in Noah's ark, this employee may be diverse and come from a very different perspective, and each of those action steps could present a huge challenge. It might require the employee to overcome many obstacles, including ignoring some of their own cultural norms. The better solution would combine the manager stepping up his actions to get the employee noticed, with the employee adapting somewhat to the organizational norms. It is crucial that the manager have a greater degree of awareness and set of tools than merely suggesting that the employee speak up as an answer to his frustration.

People come into the workplace with varying comfort levels and with behaviors that are considered the norm for any given organization. Behaviors are only norms because they have been adopted by the dominant groups in the organization, and then considered to be the right ones. Yet in a diverse, heterogeneous organization, a real danger exists—those accepted and approved actions are easier for some to follow than they are for others. If I have long been taught and encouraged by my culture to be outspoken, and the norm of the organization is to speak up, then I don't have to do much relearning or behavior shifting. However, it is much harder for me to speak up if my culture and normative behavior (my Grandma's lessons) told me *not* to stand out. Let's look at other situations that might be easy for the in-power, majority group, but harder for the out-of-power, nondominant minority groups.

GETTING NOTICED IN NOAH'S ARK

One key to a successful career is ensuring that your work gets noticed and that you actually get credit for the work you do. This might sound easy enough, but along with diversity come the differing ways in which people have learned to do or not to do this. In most organizations, an employee needs to figure out how to state their accomplishments, let their manager know what they are doing, communicate the results of their work, and even frame their mistakes in a constructive way. Good work alone does not necessarily translate to great success within an organization. This is not enough. Many people come into an organization believing if they keep their head down, work hard, and don't make a fuss, their manager will know what and how they are doing—and they expect to be rewarded accordingly. This may well be a lesson they learned at school or at home.

However, this can be a fatal error in thinking, particularly in global companies where norms differ dramatically across regions. It assumes that the manager is superhuman and gets it without being told. Some people are quite comfortable keeping their manager apprised of their work progress or successes. These types of employees aren't reluctant to share their credentials or be as straightforward in discussing their accomplishments, thus, their manager gets to know their value to the team. Others may have a Grandma who told them not to be arrogant, not to toot their own horn, and to shun self-promotion. These employees will act in a manner considered natural for them, and won't provide regular updates to their manager. They also won't map out ways in which they have helped to further the goals of the team.

Within a given company, there are often people sitting in the same room that have been brought up around very different Grandmas; and the lessons they've learned are strikingly opposing. This type of diversity can end up doing a disservice to the employees as well as to the company, unless both managers and employees learn to adjust. If those adjustments aren't made, the playing field becomes unlevel with subtle advantages for one and subtle disadvantages for the other. While some people are taught that speaking up will ultimately lead to failure, others are told that you can't get ahead unless you speak up. Here's the problem within the corporate Noah's ark.

Even though an organization may tout a desire for diversity—particularly, cognitive diversity—it may only end up with individuals from the dominant group speaking in a meeting or sharing ideas. Because of the difference in culture, relating, and expression, many employees may sit silently while only a few of their colleagues dominate the airwaves. The manager will only hear the Wheels and their accomplishments—or those who have volunteered to speak—but not the aforementioned Ducks, Nails, or the Nice. The latter are at a significant disadvantage—their careers may suffer as a result.

The company ends up losing out, since the time and effort spent on promoting workplace diversity isn't producing something beneficial, or achieving the cognitive diversity of perspective, experience, and learning.

In some cultures, people have to be asked to give their ideas, because this is what is considered the norm for them. They will respond with their ideas and thoughts once asked—but not before. This means that a manager cannot just let a discussion flow in a way that they view as natural; otherwise, the dominant groups will command all of the attention. The person leading a meeting, for example, needs to be aware of what is going on, and not immediately assume the others have nothing to say. They must act like a traffic cop, and say, "Let's hear from A; now let's hear from B; and hold on, C, D, do you have anything to add?" This is an invitation to speak, and most will respond positively to it. If this approach isn't taken, however, the manager may unconsciously credit the dominant speakers with all of the good ideas. Then, when promotion time comes, the continually aggressive speaker has the advantage—even though they may not actually have the best ideas.

The manager's conscious behavior extends even further than this. Research shows that the first or second person who speaks in a meeting actually sets the agenda; the people who speak during the first third of a meeting receive more credibility. In the previous example, the most likely people to be the first or second speaker are again those who have been taught it is okay to be the Wheel (the one who needs greasing and gets all of the attention), so once again, the goal of cognitive diversity cannot be achieved. The manager must be even more vigilant about starting a meeting with the voices and input from people other than those with the Wheel personality or viewpoint.

As mentioned, in our global world the Wheel, Nail, Duck, and Nice dynamics are most obviously experienced on a conference call—something upon which international companies must rely heavily. Remember the conference call? The individuals who are attending the conference call sit, never speaking, most often simply listening. Often, the differing time zones require that people in India or Asia be on them well past 10:00 P.M., especially if the calls have been initiated from the United States. The call moderator's request for input frequently falls flat. I've been a part of enough of these calls to know that the usual response is silence. No one speaks. The company spent millions of dollars, time, and energy on seeking this wonderful diversity—and they get *nothing* in return. Just silence.

Given how many different Grandmas we bring into our workplaces, it's difficult to achieve the true benefits of diversity. It requires management to be more aware of the way people are; what they have been taught; what they unconsciously believe about others; and how they act based on their own life's framework. In the conference call situation, the manager needs to single out individual attendees—or at least a representative group—to hear a diversity of opinions. Without this extra step and consciousness, what's the point of trying to establish the corporate Noah's ark? If you can't hear from a sampling of all of the people on board, then why bother bringing them on board at all? And when promotion time comes, the less dominant culture's carriers lose.

In some cultures, Grandma may well have told people not to speak unless whatever they say is perfectly well prepared. American style, off-the-cuff comments, or half-developed ideas leave some people very uncomfortable. One solution is to have a manager provide notice that they will be asking employees to contribute their ideas, thus allowing those who are less comfortable with this method more time to prepare. This is one way to avoid the custom of people speaking spontaneously, thus including those brought up with a Grandma who told them that was not acceptable.

Management is the institution of the organization. Every manager is in charge of a particular playing field; all of the areas under their responsibility (each of the parts) add up to be the total corporation or organization. Therefore, each manager's field must be a meritocracy if the organization as a whole is to be one. Each manager is responsible for establishing the environment that allows for true cognitive diversity — the genuinely different ideas and ways in which people think. This doesn't come easily though. Getting true value out of diversity is much harder than was initially thought, and it requires more than an MBA from its management teams.

GETTING OUT OF
YOUR OWN COMFORT ZONE

Managers aren't the only ones responsible for what happens inside an organization or company, individuals can't expect their bosses to handle everything. At some point, employees have to take it upon themselves to get out of their comfort zones and learn to adjust to a company's style, but not in a manner that merely shows compliance. There are varieties of ways for people to handle situations and become more flexible in approaching the workplace.

For example, if someone is transferred from America to Japan, he or she will benefit from toning down the squeaky wheel habit, since it will otherwise stand out and possibly offend (if not outright irritate) their new colleagues. On the other hand, the Japanese colleague who moves to the London office may need to tell Grandma to go home while learning to speak up a little more. I am not talking about *style compliance*, or taking on precisely the style of the other. This isn't ultimately effective, and it can be exhausting and unproductive to try to alter your behavior simply to mimic that of others. That said, for a person to progress in a diverse environment, they might need to find the skills to adapt slightly—to stretch a bit to their surroundings and obtain new tools and approaches, not just the ones Grandma taught them. The more tools we have, the better off we are at work.

A high-level female manager at Goldman Sachs once told me that she listens carefully to the kind of information that men and women leave for her on her voice mail. The men often identify the problem, explain what the team did about it, and then they tend to give some detail about their individual role in the solution. The women tell the manager what the problem was, what the team did about it, and usually don't include their specific role in the solution. While this particular manager notices this subtle but important difference, many others might not be so astute. Of course, this wasn't the case for *all* women or *all* men, but it was a dynamic this manager found repeated often. She was aware of how that subtle difference could magnify into unconscious performance perception.

Sociologist Pepper Schwartz says that these are more than gender issues—they are power issues. Schwartz points out that even in a room full of women, some will be more vocal than others, some will take credit for their contributions to a team effort, and others will defer to the group. "The fact that men interrupt more than women isn't because women are socialized to be less aggressive, even though that is true," says Schwartz. "The fact is that if you come to an all women's group, some women interrupt more than others. And the ones that interrupt are generally the dominant women. So, it's a power trait."

In U.S.-based corporations, we often see this power dynamic play out clearly across gender lines. A COO relayed to me that his office was on the top floor of a building, and that the corridor for his office was a dead end. If you walked to where he sat you'd have to turn around and walk back in the opposite direction. He said he was amazed at how many men seemed to be wandering by and just happened to be up there on the top floor so they could stick their head in and tell him what they were working on. This COO said no women ever happened to be "wandering by" at the end of the dead end hallway. (It's highly unlikely that men from other cultures wandered past his office door either; he only noticed and remarked on the gender difference.)

It is not unreasonable for someone to want to portray himself as having provided a significant contribution to the organization. After all, for-profit corporations are not kibbutzim or communes. They are typically hierarchies or pyramid structures — meaning there are few high-power jobs at the top and many lower-power jobs once you get further down the ladder. There is more money at the top, and less money down below; bigger offices higher up, and maybe only cubicles below. It is perfectly reasonable and perhaps even wise to portray yourself in a good light with your manager. It makes sense to let him know what you have been working on and doing it especially well. We've learned that letting people know what you do can get you ahead. (One male manager calls this "Image Management.") The problem is not that there are people who are comfortable discussing their successes. Rather, in a diverse organization the problem is that *not everyone* is comfortable doing so; and many organizations and managers forget to evaluate everyone and only use the boastful, loud Wheels as the litmus test. This naturally leaves out all of the people who were taught that speaking up and sharing your successes isn't appropriate workplace behavior.

The November 5, 2006, issue of the *New York Times* featured an article written by Kelley Holland, which describes exactly how "The Silent May Have Something to Say." Ms. Holland observes that "Tucked away among the active debaters [at a meeting] were probably a few silent employees who watched the give-and-take like a tennis match. Some of their ideas had to be at least as good as the off-the-cuff suggestions being tossed around. But they apparently sized up the situation and decided that the risk of speaking up—the chance that they would be ignored, shot down, or labeled a troublemaker—outweighed the potential benefits."

"Managers who do not seem interested in communicating can also make employees reluctant to speak about their own concerns, on anything from office atmospherics to career goals. This is particularly likely for any employee who is a minority or feels like an outsider in a work situation, like a woman in a construction company, or a 60-year-old at a start-up populated mostly by recent college graduates."

The Noah's ark diversity problem? Managers have some employees who inform them of what they are doing, and some who do not. Some people let the manager know when they sharpen their pencil well, while others assume the manager is aware when they have closed a big deal or are uncomfortable playing up their accomplishments to their superiors. The latter is often a member of the nondominant group—perhaps a woman or Asian employee—but almost certainly someone with a Grandma who has taught them a certain lesson. Then along comes a reward the manager can offer someone (because corporations are hierarchies). It might be a promotion, an unusual assignment, or a bigger client. The manager is not a bad manager, but rather his or her ingrained inclination is to give the benefit to the one who has kept them updated and subtly bragged about their work. (That's what can happen at the gym or the evening drinks ritual).

This is exactly how the playing field can become unlevel—and quite quickly. Each manager makes a subtle, unconscious decision based on various behaviors and sharing techniques. Soon enough, the organization finds that more and more men from the dominant group are being promoted because they spoke up about their work (and obeyed their Grandma). All the while, the women and men from nondominant groups end up losing opportunities and missing out on many of the promotions, because they were encouraged by their Grandmas to behave in ways that do not help them when competing with their more dominant counterparts. Then organizations are surprised to find disproportionate numbers of dominant group members at the top of the pyramid, and that the pipeline filled with nondominant group members didn't make it to the top. Subtle advantage and disadvantage are tailwinds for some and headwinds for others, because the *natural* behavior of one group is preferred to that of another.

Similar issues with diversity can crop up in career planning. Some people may be quite vocal about letting a manager know of their career goals, and talk openly about their desire to be a director, a vice president, or even a CEO. Others are rather reserved about sharing such goals because they've been taught not to share their ambitions in that way. I asked a group of Japanese women about their goals. One woman in the group had the audacity to say that she was not yet a manager, but hoped that she would be one day. She immediately put her hand to her mouth, while laughing and blushing. The other women around her did the same thing. It turns out that this woman had been incredibly bold in terms of her cultural upbringing by sharing her goals and dreams with her peers and me. Compare her hesitancy to the American man who is quite comfortable telling his manager that he would like to be promoted—and even expects that his manager will welcome hearing about his personal ambition.

The real problem lies in the manager's assumptions. He might assume the Japanese woman has no ambitions because she does not easily share them. But he knows the American man's ambitions because the man has told him. So the manager unconsciously—and quite humanly—offers the man more opportunities.

Litmus Test

The Japanese woman does start telling her manager of her ambition, similar to her male counterpart. The manager's reaction to the woman? "She's too aggressive and ambitious": Failed the litmus test. If he is comfortable with the man's behavior, he should be equally comfortable with the woman's actions.

Psychiatrist and author Anna Fels writes about men's and women's ambition in her book *Necessary Dreams*. Fels says ambition is a combination of having the skills necessary for advancement and the ability to recognize those skills. Her argument is that in most developed societies, men and women have equal access to the education required to obtain necessary skills, but that men are much more likely to receive recognition for those skills. Fels also illustrates how women are much more reluctant than men to overtly state their ambitions, even though they have ambitions that are equal to their male counterparts. Men are more comfortable asserting their desires and goals, and society is more accustomed to and comfortable with this type of expression from men than from women.

Dr. Richard Fox, associate professor of political science at Loyola Marymount University, has extensively researched the disparity between the number of men and women in elected office. In his book, *It Takes a Candidate: Why Women Don't Run for Office,* he finds that although women are less likely to run for office, when they do, they have the same chance of being elected as their male counterparts. One thing in particular stands out—men assume qualifications for elected positions, women do not necessarily view themselves as qualified for those same positions. According to Fox, men are 65 percent more likely to view themselves as qualified to run for office. More than 80 percent of men surveyed by Fox believe they are qualified for the position to which they seek election, whereas only two-thirds of the women believe themselves to be qualified. "Women may be more likely than men to doubt their qualifications to run, because they do not transfer their professional success and political exposure to their own potential candidacies," concludes Fox. He continues by indicating that the first office a woman feels she is qualified to run for is often far lower than the first office a man feels he is qualified to run for. Think school board versus Congress.

In the book *Women Don't Ask,* authors Linda Babcock and Sara Laschever illustrate how Grandma has encouraged men to be more forthright in stating exactly what they want. Simply put—they are taught to ask for what they want. Even if organizations are committed to building a meritocracy and treating diverse groups equitably, "The men will probably end up with more resources, simply because they ask for more." Babcock and Laschever found that women estimate "fair pay" to be approximately 4 percent less than what men estimate for their first jobs—and 23 percent less than men at their career-earning peak. Women say they are satisfied with their pay even when it is demonstrably less than that of a male counterpart with the same position and level of experience. It turns out that pay satisfaction correlates with pay expectations, and not with market rate or with what might be possible. In other words—we value what we expect to get, and women are typically expecting much less.

Another study discussed in *Women Don't Ask* gave male and female research subjects four dollars to count dots on a page full of pictures. The researchers told the participants to keep working until they had "earned" their four dollars. It turns out that the women worked 22 percent longer than men and counted 32 percent more dots. In another study, Babcock found that the starting salaries for women in their first postcollege jobs were six percent lower than that of men who had just graduated. Furthermore, guaranteed bonuses were 19 percent smaller for women.

These studies did not look at how salaries or bonuses are inequitable within other diverse or non-dominant groups. There are other cultures and groups for whom a sense of entitlement—or certain Grandma lessons—would lead them to ask for more, and in turn, be compensated with more. Over time, this disparity between men and women or other diverse groups in an organization will create a huge difference in lifetime earnings; and a huge difference in perception of what constitutes a meritocracy within an organization.

Babcock asserts that, "Women are less likely than men to negotiate for themselves for several reasons. First, they often are socialized from an early age" [*my term for this is Grandma*] "not to promote their own interests, and to focus instead on the needs of others. The messages girls receive—from parents, teachers, other children, the media, and society in general—can be so powerful that when they grow up, they may not realize that they've internalized this behavior; or they may realize it but not understand how it affects their willingness to negotiate. Women tend to assume that they will be recognized and rewarded for working hard and doing a good job. Second, many companies' cultures penalize women when they do ask—further discouraging them from doing so. Women who assertively pursue their own ambitions and promote their own interests may be labeled as bitchy or pushy" (my point: the manager with those perceptions failed the litmus test). Babcock goes on to explain, "These responses from women's colleagues and supervisors may *not be conscious* [my emphasis] or part of any concerted effort to 'hold women back.' More typically, they're a product of society's ingrained expectations about how women should act. As a result, women in business often watch their male colleagues pull ahead, receive better assignments, get promoted more quickly, and earn more money. Observing these inequities, women become disenchanted with their employers."

I believe that Babcock's observations about what happens to women through societal expectations also happens within other groups that are part of the corporate Noah's ark. Men and women who are in the minority—or are from other cultures that are more communal—may hesitate to ask for a higher salary or for larger bonuses. Depending on their background and which Grandma raised them, they may have been taught about being penalized when asking for too much, and that this may lead to being devalued in the workplace. It is all right when there are homogeneous norms of behavior, but diversity imbeds heterogeneous norms into the organization.

Because people have different styles, different conduct, and various ways of asking for what they want, sharing accomplishments, and interacting—it is easy to see how the diverse groups and individuals may get lost in the sea of dominant groups who are benefiting financially and professionally. If the dominant group assumes that everyone is walking in the same world, an organization—and its nondominant members—will suffer. Ironically, as I've mentioned before, unconscious handling of diversity can lead to diverse groups leaving.

CRITICAL FEEDBACK

A crucial and highly important part of a successful workplace is to provide people with critical feedback on their work. Without this pipeline, individuals can't improve or adjust their performance to meet and exceed what is expected. Professor Linda Hill of the Harvard Business School has found that there is a substantive performance gap between people given critical feedback, stretched, challenged, and mentored. Hill found that within five years, those offered feedback and given mentoring and stretch assignments will be in a far better place than those who were not—even if each of the people has started from the same position with the same skills and background. In the corporate Noah's ark, the powerful group members may well be more likely to receive the feedback, mentoring, and challenges, thereby making the nondominant, diverse groups less likely to succeed or excel because of the unconscious ways we interact with people. Their performance may suffer, due to the fact that they do not receive feedback, mentoring, or challenging assignments because they are different. People are more comfortable talking to, risking for, and mentoring someone who is like them.

One organization looked at the gap between what the manager thought the individual's performance was and the individual's own opinion of their performance. They found that the biggest gap in performance perception came from historically underrepresented groups.

Those groups believed their performance was better than the manager did. They explained that there was a real problem with communicating clearly to the employee. This was clear evidence of the "like" to "not-like" phenomenon, which is the reluctance to give feedback to someone who does not look like you and whose reaction to criticism you cannot predict.

Critical feedback is especially tricky because we are telling someone potentially negative information. A manager tends to be fairly comfortable giving critical feedback to someone who is very much like him or her. This might mean that the manager can break the ice, find commonalities, or provide reassurance that will be appreciated, understood, and heard the way the manager intended. But that same person will feel awkward, uncomfortable, and less skilled at providing feedback to a person who doesn't look like her, dress like her, or have the same Grandma. It is easy to understand this. If you are like the other, you are pretty sure you know how they will react—because you can imagine yourself in the situation and envision how you might respond. The person giving the feedback can give it without conscious thought when both people *speak* the same language. The feedback ends up being given and received in the way that it is most helpful and constructive to the individual and to the organization.

If a manager is speaking to someone from within the Noah's ark who is *not* like them, however, this natural way of being and communicating is less likely to happen.

The manager may be uncomfortable, or even worried. He could be asking himself whether the person sitting opposite him will misinterpret his comments, think he is sexist, racist, or has a beef with the employee's religion. The one who is responsible for giving the feedback may worry in advance that a woman will cry, or an African American man will get angry, or someone will file a complaint, or worse—a lawsuit. Although many of these concerns are only unconscious, the manager may still unconsciously tell the employee that he or she is doing just fine, to avoid stumbling into one of these concerns.

I was once told that the word *fine* could very well stand for "Feelings Inside Not Expressed." Often those with the least information about their performance are the most underrepresented, diverse, and nondominant groups. Imagine this scenario. There are two men in a feedback session. The manager says in a highly direct way, "You are screwing up and you just need to pull your socks up!" The man who is being reviewed is used to that kind of critical coaching. It started with his high school football coach who yelled at him in a similar fashion, so he doesn't feel threatened by that kind of interaction. While he doesn't feel worthless, he *does* hear his manager telling him that he needs to change. At the same time, the male manager does not offer much positive feedback, because he knows that the employee may actually *overhear* a compliment while downplaying or *underhearing* the criticism, much like he would.

Most men have sociologically developed a tendency called *positive allusion*—a very useful trait which means that they are likely to hear the positive about themselves first. Women, on the other hand, have a tendency to have *negative allusion*, wherein they will hear the negative about themselves initially, and internalize that. One clever study asked men to pick the body type that most closely resembled their own body type. Most men chose a body type one *better* than their own. When women were asked to do the same, they chose a body type one *worse* than their own.

Positive allusion is a great trait in terms of the confidence that it can instill. It is likely any of us could go out into the street, walk up to any man and say, "You should run for Parliament or Congress." He might straighten his tie, stand up taller, and say, "Yes, of course, what took you so long to suggest that?" Conversely, go to a woman who has been in the State legislature for 20 years and say, "You should run for Congress." She's more likely to respond that she is not ready, that she hasn't been on the right committees yet, and that she was merely lucky to win her legislative position. She says, "No, I won't be running for Congress."

A woman who gives feedback to another woman may do it in a more indirect relational fashion, because she is aware that the female employee will often *overhear* the negative and *underhear* the positive. The feedback tends to be structured more like this: "Good, good, good, good,

good, good, little bad, good, good, good, and good." Still, the manager knows that the woman will reach in, grab the "little bad," pull it out, and blow it out of proportion. She will leave her feedback session having only heard that. It is of course possible for someone to entirely mishear and misunderstand based on how you frame yourself. A senior manager once relayed a story to me about how he had told a young woman that she was doing quite well at her job, but that she would not be promoted to the next level within the year. Two days later the woman approached him in tears, wondering if this same manager was about to fire her. On the other hand, you could give most men feedback telling them that they were doing very poorly; although the last presentation to clients they made was brilliant. More often than not, they may come out of the feedback session having heard they were brilliant.

Women often don't understand how men do not hear the critical feedback about which they think they are being clear. A woman is likely to bury the criticism among the good; the bit of bad often flies right past men. Giving feedback to a man might be better heard if you just say to him, "David, you are screwing up. Pull your self together." This is something he will hear. Different cultures often respond to critical feedback based on what was expected of them growing up. Highly deferential cultures may also overhear criticism.

Linda Babcock confirms this in her research, which found that women's positive feelings about their abilities and their work performance increased substantially following positive feedback, and dropped substantially in response to negative feedback. Men's feelings about the quality of their work and themselves changed very little in response to *either* positive or negative feedback. Women develop a sense of entitlement from external reinforcement, while a man's sense of entitlement comes from within. This is how each of the groups have been encouraged and nurtured by societal norms—or by Grandma. Managers can get into trouble if they talk to women as if they were men, or to men as if they were women. If a female manager provides a man feedback in the way she would for another woman—all while hiding the bad in a cloud of good—the man may not even notice the critical feedback; whereas if a man tells a woman to "get a grip," she will likely be devastated. Managers may be misinterpreted talking to someone from a highly deferential formal culture if they are from a culture that is "boundaried" by status levels. One of the best techniques I learned in the police academy in Verbal Judo was to ask a person I'm talking with on the street, "What did you hear me say?" It is a highly effective way to ensure that the speaker and the listener are in accord with what was said during a cross-diversity encounter. For a manager, the tool might sound like, "Let's make sure you understood what I said"; for the employee, it could be "Let me make sure I understood what you said to me."

There is also the danger of the double bind in an area such as critical feedback. Kathleen Hall Jamieson's book *Beyond the Double Bind* relates classic ways that women and other nondominant groups end up being damned if they do, and damned if they don't. Let's say that during a critical feedback session, a white man gets negative commentary from another man from the same racial group. The receiver gets angry. He pushes back, gets upset, disagrees, and states his disagreement forcefully. The man providing the feedback doesn't get too upset, since he figures he probably would have reacted similarly. But the scenario changes when this same manager gives critical feedback to a woman, for example. The woman may get angry, push back, become upset, disagree, and state her position forcefully. There is a real danger that the manager will think to himself that she just can't take feedback. If she shows anger, she becomes too assertive and he may think to himself, "Bitch." On the other hand, the woman has just received feedback that upsets her. Grandma taught her that it is okay for a woman to cry when upset; so she cries. That unnerves the manager even more, and he starts thinking that she is too emotional and weak. Do you see the double bind here? She is too assertive if she gets angry and too weak if she cries. That is why she's damned if she does, and damned if she doesn't.

To be fair, men have a single bind. They are permitted to get angry, but if they express frustration or anger through tears, they may face far greater humiliation or the possibility of being penalized just for showing their emotions. Of course, this doesn't happen in all situations, but it is important to recognize the consequences of these learned behaviors and responses in any place in the world.

Generally, men can get angry in the workplace and not pay the same penalty that is incurred by women who express their irritation at work. A recent study from Yale University revealed that the salary of an angry man was approximately $38,000, while the angry woman was making $23,500. "When women express anger at work, no matter what they do on the job, they can be seen as 'out of control' or are viewed in a negative light," says study author, Victoria Brescoll. It is almost expected for men to get angry. As a negative stereotype that is reinforced, their colleagues usually get over the outburst they witnessed. The angry male employee may not get away with his behavior, but he isn't likely to suffer long-term consequences or labeling the way an angry female will.

When other individuals from nondominant groups get angry, or act in a way that is not expected, they too will be judged more harshly. The study made it clear that a man who gets irate at work may well be admired for it, while a woman who shows such emotion in the workplace is liable to be seen as out of control and incompetent. There are archetypal perceptions about angry men from various racial or ethnic backgrounds that could play an unconscious role here as well. The angry black man is an archetype that can be severely damaging to the African American individual who bears the brunt of someone's unconscious beliefs. This differing reaction to anger can be tested anywhere in the world with the "hot-headed" perception for one group against the dominant group reaction.

WHO APOLOGIZES AND WHO INTERRUPTS

Seemingly small social interactions in the workplace can have huge impacts. Women and others from nondominant groups have been taught by Grandma to do ritual apologizing while trying to make others feel good or feel equal. While it's common to hear women saying, "I'm sorry" quite frequently, it does not mean that they have actually made a mistake. Rather, it is a relating technique and a ritual, which usually is easily recognized—even subconsciously—by other women. One woman says, "I'm sorry" and the other woman says, "Oh, I'm sorry too," and then each is content and moves on. Very often, neither woman interpreted the "sorry" as evidence that the other had made a mistake in this mutually satisfying exchange.

Men in many cultures are less likely to be ritual apologizers, since this can be seen as putting oneself below the other or getting into a weaker position in relation to the other. Therefore, it is not common to hear the, "I'm Sorry. I'm Sorry Too" exchange between two men as you would with two women. In the workplace, if women fall unconsciously into the "I'm sorry" routine with a man, it may be perceived as weakness, even though it is in fact merely a ritual or a learned habit.

There is the empathy response and the "this happened to me too" response. The *Wall Street Journal* once told the story of two women speaking about an accident that one of them had. The other woman wants to know if she is okay, if anyone was hurt, and sympathizes with how terrible it sounds. When the women told a male colleague about the accident, his first response was to tell her that a similar situation had just happened to him. She finds him unsympathetic—even though *he* thinks he has just told her how much he can empathize with her situation. These *Men Are from Mars, Women Are from Venus*-type situations can be considered humorous or just frustrating at home or while on a date. However, these interactions can be downright dangerous in the diverse workplace where the power, position, and money lie with one or the other person—each judging the other by their own ritual speaking patterns.

Interrupting is another unconscious pattern. In some cultures, ritual interrupting is considered fine and carries no negative social consequence. In other cultures—and often for women—Grandma teaches that you stop talking when interrupted by someone else. That might be fine in a nightclub, at home, or in a social setting, but the workplace is supposed to offer a professional opportunity for an exchange of ideas and ultimately rewards are attached. Those subtle interactions—including the habitual interrupting of someone that leads them to stop talking—can actually create problems for an organization or company.

For example, if an American man interrupts an Indian man, the latter has likely been taught by Grandma to let the other speak—especially if seniority or hierarchy is involved. The Indian man had ideas to offer, but stops himself from saying anything and ends up not sharing at all because the American man has taken over the conversation. Two negative elements have occurred. First, the Indian employee's ideas are lost, and gone with those is the cognitive diversity essential to a successful global company. Second, the American man now is being heard over the Indian man, and he receives the managerial attention and consideration that is no longer given to his colleague.

Managers need to be constantly aware of these small dynamics within the corporate Noah's ark. It seems simple, yet these unhealthy patterns are repeated on a daily basis for years at a time. A successful manager must be hyperaware in a way that isn't as necessary when dealing with a homogeneous group. The manager—and the employees—will benefit from intervening and saying, "Hold on John, let Ramesh finish." And Ramesh will have to push himself to get outside of his comfort zone and learn to say, "John, I want to hear what you have to say (a way to keep the relationship intact), but do let me finish." This is not a cocktail party. This is a corporate hierarchy, within which small interactions can have a lasting and significant impact.

MENTORING

As we learned from Linda Hill's research, employees will thrive and work will improve when they are presented with assignments that stretch their abilities, when they are given critical feedback, and when they receive mentoring. Mentoring is crucial for everyone, but in Noah's ark, not everyone receives it, nor does everyone receive it equitably. Harvard Business School professor David Thomas has done extensive research on corporate mentoring, with a particular focus on how it impacts people of color. He looks at how beliefs, unarticulated perceptions, archetypes, and assumptions about race can quickly make an organization an unfair place. Diversity is a particular challenge to the mentoring process, and Thomas focuses on several crucial reasons why mentoring across diversity can be problematic. Cross race and gender are his focus; however, my belief is that these cross-diversity issues arise between groups based on differences such as language skills, nationalities, body types, and marital status. All of these characteristics or traits are a potential hurdle to the ideal mentoring situation.

Let's take a look at the mentoring pitfalls addressed by Thomas.

Negative stereotypes. Mentors who don't look like their mentees have to give their charges the benefit of the doubt that they can succeed. This can be much harder than it sounds. Although unconscious, the mentor may harbor a tentative opinion about a certain person's abilities based solely on what the other person looks like. Will the mentee prove herself worthy of the investment of time and energy that the mentor is expected to provide? A mentee that looks like her mentor will be less likely to start with a deficit in that relationship. A mentor may initially assume that their mentee is worthy of their time and effort, unless of course she proves otherwise.

Mirroring. If the mentor sees a version of himself when he was young in his new mentee, then he will react with more tolerance and enthusiasm. The mentor will more quickly empathize with mistakes or blunders. He will be more apt to coax and guide in ways that may have been helpful to him years earlier. This mirroring encourages more risk taking on the part of the mentor and mentee.

Getting close. Forming a close bond or relationship can be particularly challenging across gender boundaries. Mentoring can happen in many places and through various forms. Sometimes mentors take their mentees to dinner or drinks, play a round of golf, or sit quietly behind closed doors. However, if a male mentor is taking a young female to dinner or drinks to get to know her better, this may be misconstrued or seem downright inappropriate. However, bonding with another male at a local bar is seen as perfectly acceptable, and these shared experiences allow the bond between the mentor and mentee to become quite strong. Mentors who are paired with mentees who look and act nothing like them will stand out. If the middle-aged, gay man is mentoring a young man, the pair may potentially be the subject of others' misunderstanding.

Risk. Anyone who takes on the job of mentoring is taking on a significant risk. A mentor puts her own reputation on the line, as if she has just placed a bet on a specific horse at the racetrack. The mentor wants the mentee to succeed. But if a dominant group mentor is working with a nondominant mentee, the visibility of failure is much higher for both people involved. There is much less risk associated with mentoring the young person who looks like you, because if your mentee fails, people won't be wondering from the sidelines why you took on (in their minds) a less capable person.

Resentment by others. "Like to like" mentoring happens constantly—informally over drinks, on the tennis courts, walking down the hall, popping into someone's office for a quick chat, or sitting together at lunch. Because these are casual encounters, they are not typically identified as "mentoring"; and in fact may not even be noticed at all. But when two people look nothing alike, or share none of the same outside interests, and they are having lunch, chatting in the hallway, and wandering off together during a retreat—others will take notice. Others will wonder why that manager is spending so much time with that person and not with them. Though this resentment may occasionally occur in like to like relationships, it is much more likely to be noticed and remarked upon in like to not like relationships. Men may explain their hesitation to mentor women because of the fear that people will misconstrue the mentoring dinner as something else. You can see, however, how this can unlevel the playing field for the woman who does not get that important mentoring relationship.

Even those who have the potential to be strong and productive mentors can find that their natural reaction is to resist mentoring those who don't look like them. The dominant zebra or elephant prefers to stick to its own kind, rather than try to figure out the puzzle that exists in working with the squirrel. Simultaneously, mentors are an excellent resource for young employees to learn the ropes, get to know a corporate culture, and decipher the unwritten rules of an organization. These two elements collide to create a disproportionate spread of knowledge, and subtle advantages to those who continue to look like the people at the top, or those in charge of an organization. Therefore, we have no reason to be surprised when those who don't look like the dominant group fall behind. In spite of all of the processes in place—the language of diversity, the meritocracy that the organization uses in its mission statements, and the mentoring systems—the unconscious and natural behavior will undermine it all.

However, it is *not* diversity that undermines meritocracy; but rather the fact that with diversity comes many Grandmas' societal norms who come to work with us and who have taught us to think, act, and believe in certain ways.

It is not necessarily easy for someone to state naturally their accomplishments in the same manner as their peers. It is a challenge to speak up and be noticed or to communicate ideas when you were taught *not* to do so during your formative years. It requires courage to share your ambitions and goals when there are social consequences for doing so, even though you will harm yourself in your career if you don't. Diverse organizations require much more conscious planning, implementation, awareness, interaction, and evaluation than most of the people at the top realize. Well-meaning diversity efforts will remain just that if organizations fail to understand that what's easy for some is truly hard for others.

Chapter 5

Unwritten Rules

Think about the first time you took your partner or significant other to your parents' home. What did you warn her about? What did you tell him to say—or *not* say? You probably wanted the first meeting to go smoothly—you were the one who knew the family dynamic, customs, habits, and the traps for the unwary. You know what your mother thinks about people who dress a certain way, or how your father will evaluate your partner's worth based on his opinions concerning sports.

Before you arrive, you might make statements like, "Make sure you compliment my father's spaghetti sauce and meatballs," or "Please don't wear that worn out sweater, because it will make my mother feel disrespected." Maybe you suggested that your partner avoid talking about religion or politics or a particular Hollywood star. "Hug my mother," you suggest. "Shake hands with my father." These are the types of unwritten rules that you want to impart to your partner before he or she unknowingly makes a fatal mistake—one that could have easily been avoided.

Organizations have just as many unwritten rules as families do. An individual's success in a given company will largely be determined by how quickly they learn these rules, and whether they learn them at all. A new employee or manager can make mistakes they didn't even know were considered mistakes, and not all of these blunders are the same from organization to organization. An employee is at a great advantage if a seasoned manager or coworker gives her information on the firm's understood policies. But if you don't have someone who passes along the dos and don'ts, you're often at a serious disadvantage early on. You can end up committing a major faux pas—and may never make up for the seemingly innocent act.

Imagine that your company transfers you to Cairo, and no one bothers to tell you that in Egypt, it is rude to eat with your left hand or show the soles of your shoes; that you shouldn't extend your hand to a man if you are a woman; that it is entirely appropriate for men to walk hand in hand; and that you should always defer to the most senior person in a room. If violated, these are unwritten rules that could create a negative impression. In turn, you may end up having to expend time and energy overcoming and apologizing.

Similarly, if a boss has a real problem with flip-flops or sandals in an otherwise casual environment, it's better to be told this up front than to find out that your reputation has somehow been compromised for wearing the wrong shoes. Everyone benefits if told about these customs, expectations, and unwritten rules in advance. In Noah's ark, it is essential that this kind of teaching be done for everyone, and not just for the like to like people. It is natural for people to get comfortable more quickly with people who are like them. Therefore, it's important that the manager not only give out advice and tips to the new employees who are like her, but also to everyone she manages. This way, each employee will start off with the same knowledge and advantage.

Consider the following four scenarios in which unwritten rules come into play:

1. Imagine that the CEO of your new organization is quite formal, and expects his employees to be the same. However, in your former job, it was acceptable to walk around the office without your suit jacket. Now, when you go without your jacket, you are considered to be quite informal, and have actually been marked as someone who is unprofessional.

2. What if your manager likes to tell jokes, starts meetings with small talk about family, and wants you to relate to her in an informal way? But perhaps, due to your culture, you are used to hierarchies. You've been taught that formal titles—Mr. or Ms.—are important, while personal chatter or bantering is considered

disrespectful. Or you are gay, not out and not sure how your sexual orientation plays out in organizational acceptance, so you don't join in on that small talk about family.

3. Imagine that your organization hosts town hall-style meetings at which the president encourages people to ask questions. One day you do—only to find out later that the president doesn't want spontaneous questions. That's not the way it *actually* works.

4. Let's say that during meetings, the senior leaders are aggressive in stating their opinions—so much so that it feels to you as though they are arguing. They verbally spar, shout over each other, and even insult one another. You were brought up with the understanding that raising your voice is never allowed, and such confrontation is considered unacceptable behavior.

As you can see from these examples, there needs to be a guide to help individuals navigate the culture of an organization in order to succeed. This is especially true if the individual has been brought on to help complete the corporate Noah's ark. We unconsciously bring whatever we learned or were comfortable with from other organizations. We also bring our family dynamics, our understanding of proper behavior that we learned from our religion or the classroom, or the attitudes and roles we've adopted from the movies we watch. Without that guide or mentor who tells you the unwritten rules and thinks, "You remind me of me when I was young and I want to make sure you succeed," you may be at a significant disadvantage—without even knowing it.

SUBTLE INEQUITIES

A Massachusetts Institute of Technology (MIT) study looked at why women professors were not getting the same number of tenure appointments as men. What was discovered were subtle inequities, or—in the language of diversity literature—small actions that, over time, either subtly advantage or disadvantage different members of the workplace. The actions that lead up to an inequity may be so small that they are largely undetected and hard to pinpoint. Individuals may not even notice the inequities, or if they do, it may seem petty to bring them up. In the case of advantage, the subtlety may be so embedded in an interaction that it is no longer even done consciously.

Subtle inequities are particularly harmful in Noah's ark, because certain groups will traditionally be advantaged or disadvantaged despite an organization's best attempts at making the evaluative process merit based. An example of an action that has subtle implications is a person simply glancing at their computer screen or BlackBerry. Imagine that a manager's golfing buddy who works under him comes into his office to discuss a matter.

The manager gives the person his full attention, greeting the person warmly, talking a few minutes about last week's round of golf, and then takes the time to listen to the employee and respond accordingly. Sounds good, right?

Now imagine that the employee who has something to discuss looks nothing like his manager. In Noah's ark, the difference stands out; and when you walk into the office of someone who is different from you, you are more apt to be hesitant and worry that you are a burden to your manager. Similarly, the manager may not feel the need to give this person—who is unlike him—as much attention as the more familiar guy. This is probably not conscious behavior, since few managers intentionally create inequities. Though the manager is initially listening to his employee, he is distracted, and instinctively glances at his computer. That simple glance conveys a powerful message to his subordinate—a sign of disrespect or lack of interest. The employee who is talking will feel marginalized, as if he is taking too much of his manager's time or has nothing important to say. Ultimately, the manager hasn't listened well and the employee comes away feeling as though the manager doesn't value him as highly as the golfing buddy.

This will all come back to haunt and hurt an organization. It's a wonder to me that corporate leaders are actually *surprised* when employee surveys reveal that diverse individuals are not typically as satisfied and don't feel as valued as the dominant groups. For the nondominant group, this often creates an environment in which their work suffers; they receive less favorable reviews; and they ultimately leave because they are frustrated with the lack of feedback they've received. There goes the company's cognitive diversity, and its allegedly level playing field.

Consider the following examples of important subtle inequities:

- Imagine there is a manager introducing two people from his team to a new client. Jim, the manager, is a white male. David, a member of the team, is his frequent tennis partner. Rose, a Latino woman, joined Jim's team two years ago, but has never really been in Jim's inner circle.

  > "Let me introduce you to David, who is a great strategic thinker and an important part of our team," says Jim. "And this is Rose, whom we are pleased to have on our team." I'm sure you catch the subtle difference in how David's and Rose's credentials are presented. No doubt, Rose comes away feeling somewhat underappreciated.

- Giving women or other nondominant groups less feedback, fewer critical comments, and engaging in less frequent informal water cooler chats is a form of subtle inequity. Without these interactions, the nondominant individuals are likely to be integrated into the company—or onto a team—at a much slower pace, or worse, promoted more slowly. Their performance may suffer.

- If a senior executive visits a divisional office and walks down the center aisle of the office greeting those who happen to sit there or those whom he knows, he will miss out on interacting with most of the company's personnel. In order to effectively talk with and observe a sampling of employees, an executive should instead make the effort to visit various areas of the office—especially out-of-the-way corners and those with whom he feels he has less in common.

- When women and other historically underrepresented groups ask questions, they are often perceived as lacking knowledge or confidence. However, when dominant group members ask questions, they are deemed curious and interested. It's crucial to watch that we don't make these assumptions that drive easily avoidable subtle inequities.

- As seen, subtle inequities result from not noticing who is being interrupted or who interrupts, and failing to intervene to make the situation fair for everyone. Nondominant group members may not try to share their opinions again if they have already been interrupted—unless they are specifically called upon. Some may feel that they have to raise their hand

and be asked to speak while others continue shouting out unsolicited comments. This creates an unequal dynamic.

- These inequities can also stem from managers who expect one woman to answer for or represent all women. Simultaneously, it is unfair to think that one Asian person represents the perspective of all Asians. This dynamic can be seen in conversations during which a manager turns to a woman and says, "What do women think about that?"

- Others include:

    Not pronouncing foreign names correctly

    Seating your buddies next to you at the meeting

    Making eye contact with some and not others

    Apologizing to the women in the room if you swear

    Giving certain people better or bigger accounts and projects while overlooking others

    Always favorably commenting on the input of certain individuals but not on others

As unintended as they usually are, people read into these actions a great deal, and feelings of inclusion or exclusion can readily occur.

The MIT research shows that over time, these subtle inequities can significantly disadvantage some groups, while providing dramatic rewards to others; and as previously discussed, those in the position of advantage are often completely unaware of their inherent privilege. Because things are going well for them and they are treated fairly, they are often overwhelmingly convinced that their organization is a meritocracy. Why *wouldn't* it be a fair and equitable place to work? After all, they worked hard and got to the top. Of course they think there is a level playing field for everyone.

In those focus groups I mentioned in the introduction with white American men, women, minorities, and non-Americans, it was as if they were living in different worlds—certainly working in different corporations. I remember the women believing that there was still an old boy's network in place. One said, "Decisions are made in a smoke-filled room." When I shared this particular comment with management, one of the executives was pretty upset. "How could that possibly be?" he asked. "We have a no smoking policy in the company offices."

Again, the American minorities thought that the whole diversity effort was driven by legal requirements and the Equal Employment Opportunity Commission standards. The EEOC is the agency of the United States federal government that enforces federal employment discrimination laws. The non-Americans said that it was almost impossible to run the company if you weren't from the company's corporate headquarters. You might be able to run the New Delhi office if you were from India, but have little chance of being asked to join the management team in the office at the American headquarters.

What this suggests is that most of us are not fully aware of what goes on in our corporate lives, or how we might be at a subtle advantage. Those who have been historically underrepresented or who are members of nondominant groups are usually aware of their own subtle—or not-so-subtle—disadvantages. Many African Americans know what it's like to have a taxicab driver not stop for them. Other dark-skinned women know what it is like to be followed in a department store by someone who suspects them of shoplifting. Over time, these subtle but significant experiences have a strong impact on who we are and how we act in the world.

Diversity consultant Kendall Wright talks about "possibility and frequency." He is referring to the fact that it is possible that any one of us could have a taxi drive by without stopping when we hail it. But the frequency with which it happens to someone based on skin color varies dramatically: Once for some people, but many times for others; and there is usually a long-term effect if you continue to fall prey to these subtle inequities. Subtle inequities can either advantage or disadvantage; subtle disadvantages are penalizing and put *the other* on a slower trajectory with fewer rewards. Harvard Business School professor David Thomas reflects on the slower trajectory of women and minorities in organizations when compared to the dominant group. Diverse people get discouraged, perceive themselves as less valued, reduce confidence in themselves, and often end up with lower productivity and performance—because they were not given the same advantages that historically overrepresented groups are given.

We walk in different worlds based on who we are, what Grandma taught us, and what we have experienced in our lives. It is almost understandable how those with subtle advantages forget about the needs of those who are subtly disadvantaged. Take New York Governor David Patterson, who is legally blind. When he took office following then-Governor Eliot Spitzer's resignation in 2008, Patterson immediately had the state's web site changed to offer a larger font size for the visually impaired. It's a small gesture that will go a long way for many. However, most of us without vision impairments would never have thought to implement such a change. If I had been sitting on a deserted island for 10 years, I don't think it would have occurred to me to offer that. Yet this differing worldview is precisely the point of cognitive diversity.

Liberian President Ellen Johnson-Sirleaf talked with me about the qualities that women can bring to leadership and elected office—issues upon which men have not traditionally been focused. "They bring to the task a different dimension of sensitivity; sensitivity that may conflict with what the normal decision ought to be," says Johnson-Sirleaf. "A woman leader decided that, I believe in the welfare of children, for example." Yet these same women who are bringing cognitive diversity to the table are being judged for bringing different ideas that may compete with the status quo.

It is often difficult for dominant groups to get into the shoes of the members of less powerful groups. It is indeed hard to imagine someone else's perspective, or have a sense of another person's obstacles or concerns. But the health and success of an organization requires that those at the top—those from the influential groups—consciously attempt to see things from other perspectives, if not seek them out and listen closely to them. Managing diversity requires heightened emotional intelligence, awareness, observation, and listening skills.

Organizations must get beyond diversity by being conscious and aware that there are many unwritten rules in their organizations. Some people are informed of them while others aren't—for all sorts of reasons—in Noah's ark. If these are not communicated to all, then those who don't receive this coaching will have a disadvantage that may work against them for their entire careers.

Chapter 6

We Hire for Difference and Fire Because They Are Not the Same

THE DANGER OF UNCONSCIOUS THINKING, SPEAKING, AND ACTING

Speech patterns are one of the most automatic habits that we learn during our childhood. For each of us, the way we speak is the right way, because it is the only way we know. Our language is natural—at least to ourselves. Yet others learn their *own* ways that may be quite different from our own. In a diverse organization, we often ignore all of these different speech patterns and language habits at our own peril. It reminds me of the song lyric, "You say tomato, I say tomahto; let's call the whole thing off." I saw the title of this chapter tacked to a bulletin board during a session on diversity. No author was noted, but it certainly stuck with me. That said, we shouldn't feel compelled to call it off just because we may be forced to grapple with difference in Noah's ark.

I learned the danger of transferring the unconscious habits of operating in a workplace quite different from my familiar corporate one (where I've worked for 25 years) when I took on a new role several years ago. As I mentioned in the introduction, after the attacks of September 11, I decided that I wanted to become a first responder. I was in New York City on that terrible morning, and my feelings of helplessness were overwhelming. I had previously worked in the airline industry and was trained in disaster recovery in case of an airplane crash—this was far beyond anything I had been taught to tackle.

So I joined the Metropolitan Police Reserve Corps in Washington, DC. In order to qualify, we were sent to the police academy for 10 months of training—after which I became a police officer and perhaps, as I say, the oldest living female mountain bike officer. I learned an incredible amount in the academy, but one lesson that stands out most took place when an instructor warned us right from the beginning that our most dangerous weapon is not our service weapon, but rather, our words. The things we say unconsciously have the potential to get us—and others—into the most amount of trouble in the least amount of time. Words spoken *consciously* can also get us and others *out* of trouble just as quickly—if we speak intentionally and mindfully.

The idea is that if we each merely spoke, reacted, and acted naturally, we would likely find ourselves getting into tough—and potentially dangerous—situations. Instead, we were asked to learn a new form of speaking called Verbal Judo. George Thompson, an English professor and police officer who has taught this method at many police academies around the country, developed this technique. Verbal Judo is a means of using language to get someone to comply voluntarily with your original request. Unpleasant confrontations are more likely to occur if an officer talks, without conscious thought, to someone on the street. "Stop doing what you are doing! Get over here now! Stay calm and be reasonable!" These are all natural ways to speak in a tense and difficult situation. However, by using a demanding voice or loaded words, you may only further escalate the tension, which could result in violence.

It's no wonder, then, that an individual who has been yelled at by a police officer would turn around and start cursing at the officer, even making derogatory remarks about the officer's mother. Once riled up, they may start moving around in unpredictable and threatening ways. Once someone starts acting or speaking abnormally or becomes threatening, we've been instructed on how to use an appropriate level of force when justified, even up to nonlethal weapons like pepper spray or a baton if the circumstances move to that level. I've been pepper sprayed at the police academy, and it's simply not pleasant. Anything we can do to avoid this or the use of any weapon is certainly preferable.

So we learned how to avoid this unconscious kind of speaking by relying on Verbal Judo, which seeks voluntary compliance through a deliberate way of speaking that's actually quite unnatural to most of us. For example, we were instructed to say, "For your safety and mine, you need to stop doing what you are doing." Depending on the situation, we may say, "Is there anything else I can say or do to get you to do A, B, or C?" or, "I would like to help you here, so let's talk through what just happened." We were also taught to give people options. "You can stop doing what you're doing, or here is another option: I will put you in this police car, take you to the station, and book you. You will probably miss work tomorrow. Or remember the other option—you can stop doing what you are doing." These are more engaging, less threatening methods of interacting, but they definitely take practice and deliberate, conscious thought.

In the corporate workplace, we speak in ritual ways that we don't even realize are routine and unconscious. We tend to react based on what we are familiar with, and how we are accustomed to saying something, and not at all based on how someone else in Noah's ark might speak or act. It can feel nearly impossible to get outside of our own worldview and see the perspective and language patterns of another without reacting negatively to the difference.

Consider this simple interaction between colleagues at work:

> "Hi, how are you?"
> "I'm fine. How are you?"
> "I'm fine, thanks."

This is an incredibly common exchange in the American workplace. Yet if we observe it consciously, neither speaker is asking a genuine question or looking for an honest answer. This is not a request for information. Most of us know what it's like when someone actually answers the question and starts to talk about their sick daughter, how their cat just died, or their demanding boss. The listener thinks, "Whoa. Stop! I wasn't really asking!" It's likely we would be put off by having to hear too much information, or think it's strange that the other person just opted to blab on—since we weren't truly asking for that. Typically, Americans know and respect the ritual, and think nothing of using it as a friendly but quick greeting.

But, let's say you are from Russia, where such a ritual interaction doesn't exist. A Russian man once told me that he was shocked when someone asked him how he was, because it's simply not done where he is from. Another person told me that "How are you?" is a genuine question that is asked in order to solicit significant—rather than superficial—information. This woman was shocked by what she saw as insincere, rude behavior by Americans—given how they responded to that question. To her, the lack of information provided in response to "How are you?" was insulting, as was the way in which someone keeps walking while saying, "Hi. How are you?" Because all of these people bring along their own rituals, beliefs, and Grandmas, this simple exchange—and the reactions to it—can be interpreted in a variety of ways. This seemingly innocuous exchange can be quite loaded for those sharing space in Noah's ark.

In a given organization, a manager who has different rituals may well interpret the employees' practices as something other than right—and evaluate that person negatively—because it is not how they would have said or handled it.

Author and linguist Deborah Tannen writes extensively about the ritualistic expression, "Where are you going?" that is often asked in the Philippines. As she points out, we make conclusions about people based on how they interact with us, react to our questions, and engage in conversation. If you were to answer this question in the Philippines with actual information, people would find it odd and off-putting. This is a simple greeting in the Philippines, not actually an inquiry about your destination. It is not at all like when the American asks, "Where are you going?"; a real request for information.

In China, the ritual question that plays a similar role is often, "Have you eaten?" I heard this quite frequently in China. At first, I thought I'd be taken to lunch once I said that I hadn't—and continued to be hungry once I realized that it wasn't going to happen! Unfortunately, I had it all wrong. In China, the polite way of responding—whether you've just finished a meal or are ravenously hungry—is to say, "Yes I have, thank you, and have you eaten?" I know many first-timers to China think the Chinese are obsessed with eating because of how frequently they pose this ritual question.

Another simple example of this is the word "yes." In most cultures, it means "affirmative," "I agree," or "deal done." But not in Japan, where it simply means: "I heard you. I acknowledge you just spoke." *Or*—the individual takes in a deep breath, and says "yes." You have actually just been told very loudly that the answer is indeed *no*. The deal is *not* done. In Saudi Arabia, your client may say, "Yes" to you, and you think you've closed the negotiations. But, then he may tell you a story about a Bedouin in the desert. While you are confused by the relevancy of the story, the Saudi Arabian is presenting you with a strong "No" that is subtly embedded within the story.

In the corporate Noah's ark, it is essential that we become more aware of how the different Grandmas can impede the same diversity that is supposed to ensure that everyone is evaluated fairly. We must work consciously to see that there is transparency in place, so that we don't allow our different Grandmas to overpower the same systems that are supposed to provide for meritocracies. If the organization merely adds diversity as part of its mission, it will create subtle and unconscious actions and reactions. Instead, we must go beyond diversity to understand that, unless it is approached with mindful care, such a goal will continue to challenge rather than reward us.

Men and women are often caught in patterns of speech that are difficult for the other to comprehend or manage. Much of Tannen's groundbreaking work focuses on the different ways in which the two genders communicate. Females tend to be indirect speakers, while males are more often direct. Neither is right or wrong; Grandma just encouraged women to speak in certain patterns, and men to speak in others.

Whenever I travel abroad, I ask if the women speak differently than the men, and no matter where I am, the answer is always yes. This difference may be seen in a variety of ways, such as word order, deferential level, number of words, tone, levels of informal or formal speak, and the types of words used. Gendered speech patterns are neither correct nor incorrect; they are merely the way in which the individuals were encouraged to speak.

Indirect speakers are more likely to focus on the relationships between and among the people engaged in a conversation. Self-deprecating comments—ensuring that everyone is included, and focusing less on hierarchy—are rituals often included in this pattern. As Deborah Tannen points out, indirect speech patterns may also include conditional wording, mitigation or ritual humility, or open-ended phrasing instead of declarative, definitive statements. The intent of this style is to allow everyone in on the conversation, and may include lengthy explanations about thinking and details on process. Rather than sharing their own credentials, the indirect speaker relies on their spoken expertise and shared details. This language pattern will sometimes reveal how a person feels about what is being said.

For example, a woman might e-mail her manager to alert him on an issue. She tells it like a story about a relationship. "John came to me today to tell me his wife is sick and hadn't finished his briefing report. He was really upset and I tried to calm him down. I wondered whether this was just another excuse as he has missed deadlines before, and though I believe he is telling the truth, I am not sure about how to handle it. I did talk to him. I don't want to bother you but do you have any ideas on this one?"

The male manager probably stopped reading after the "Once upon a time" beginning. The woman actually does know how to handle it but wants to include her boss. The manager wonders why she isn't just reporting to him the following: (1) Briefing report late. (2) John's work is in question. (3) I have handled it in this way....

For those who grew up with Grandma encouraging direct speech, however, indirect speech and the e-mail example can be perceived as rambling or inconclusive, and the person talking may come across as unsure of their position and priorities. In actual conversation, indirect speaking might sound something like, "I feel that we might want to consider this approach, but I am not sure; we might want to discuss another approach, depending on what everyone else thinks." There are levels of ritual modesty, invitations for others to add ideas, concern for the relationship, and a desire not to sound too forceful. All of this is transmitted by the speaker using this style of speech.

Direct speaking is more transactional and focused on the information being transmitted, rather than the reactions or impact on the relationships. Direct speakers tend to use a succinct sentence structure with fewer words, almost no ritual modesty, substantial credentialing, and a strong communication of assurance. And they usually reach conclusions quickly and will provide the backstory if asked. Information is typically presented as bulleted priorities that require minimal explanation: "I have three things to say." The direct speaker often assumes that if someone wants additional information or a more comprehensive explanation, they will simply ask for it. But for those who were taught by Grandma to be indirect speakers, this type of direct speaking can feel cold and exclusionary. It seems to them as though the speaker is bulldozing his audience, is unwilling to have a discussion, and is not open to input or new ideas from others.

Tannen discusses the tendency of men to talk in a "one up/one down" fashion, which involves one person on the top and one on the bottom. One wins; the other loses. One is in the power position, and the other is not. In the workplace, men are more likely to banter with other men, rather than with women; and women are less inclined to banter with anyone. Evidence even points to women feeling less comfortable with this type of one up/one down interaction, even with other women, since they tend to feel as though it may even damage their relationships, or be seen as rude and hurtful. I call this banter "verbal towel slapping." After all, much more towel slapping occurs in boys' locker rooms than in girls'.

Here's an e-mail exchange between two DC male reserve police officers on which I was copied. One of the men, named Rodger, received an e-mail from another officer about a work issue. In the middle of the e-mail stream the other officer wrote, "Why do you have that stupid 'd' in your name?" Barely pausing, Rodger's e-mail replied, "As the tattoo on her lower back suggests, your mama loves my name." Another officer on the e-mail stream jumped into the exchange and exclaimed, "We have a winner." This type of banter that men often display is the epitome of the winner/loser exchange. It was perfect one up/one down dynamic and the men were not only unfazed by it; they seemed really to enjoy it. Watch any guy-type Hollywood movie or listen at the start of a meeting with a group of American men and you will hear plenty of this verbal put-down banter. Actually, I use it a lot when I'm working as a reserve police officer with my predominantly male colleagues. I admit it; it is kind of fun.

Many women can't understand how two men in a meeting can be going at it with each other, talking in a heated fashion, criticizing each other's ideas—and then be having a drink at the bar together 30 minutes later. Two women sparring like that in a meeting? That's a six-month repair job. The women would take it personally;

whereas men claim that it isn't personal, brush it off, and absorb the interaction as part of business. For them, it is a game, and there will be another one tomorrow if this one is lost today. Some cultures may not encourage this casual bantering, which means that there are varying levels of comfort about the tone of interactions where there is diversity.

Both transactional and relational styles are important, and too much of one or the other can actually be harmful. Direct and indirect speaking patterns are just that—speaking patterns. The best communicators learn to use both as tactics of speech and interaction, and can adjust seamlessly depending on the situation. If, for example, I am on the street and approach someone as a uniformed reserve police officer, I may say, "Do you live around here or work around here?" I begin by allowing the conversation to be slightly more relational. If the person disrespects my partner or me, then I switch the language to more transactional and direct.

Of course, men and women don't always comply with these speech patterns. Although we have natural ways of speaking that divide down gender lines, you may find a man who doesn't speak directly, or a woman who speaks quite directly. For example, I spent more than three hours with British Prime Minister Margaret Thatcher while interviewing her for my book and video documentary *Women World Leaders.* As I mentioned in my Introduction, she was told that women have an unconscious tendency to lift their voices at the end of sentences, making it sound as if they are asking a question. Even when women aren't asking a question, this common pattern has become a ritual of speaking. The unconscious purpose is to invite others into the conversation rather than sound overly dominant. But Thatcher also noted that when men hear a woman's voice lift at the end of a sentence, they hear a question; then wonder why the woman has no confidence in what she is saying. "Why is she asking a question?" they wonder. Imagine hearing, "My name is Laura?" with an upward tick at the end sounding like a question. A man is more likely to think, "Doesn't she know her name?" If you listen closely to Thatcher speak, you'll notice that she doesn't have this inflection. She is also known for speaking quite directly, like men, and uses few conditional words. Interestingly, I have noticed that when men watch my video documentary of my interviews with women presidents and prime ministers, they typically lean forward, sit up straighter, and listen closely when Thatcher is speaking.

One example in my film is when Thatcher says quite forcefully, "Life is not fair. If you think it is, you are sorely mistaken. What you've got to do in politics is be sure that what you say can be justified by principle, by argument, and to put it across. As I always say, never follow the crowd. Make up your own mind and get the crowd to follow you." Not one conditional, ritually modest word in the statement, and she even included a three-point emphasis in her sentence structure. If used consciously, this is a tool for persuasive speaking.

Lady Thatcher had remarkably adopted her rituals to match those of the dominant group, and had in turn figured out how to harness some of the ritualistic differences floating around Noah's ark. Thatcher essentially adopted the coloration of the species she was trying to invade. Until you get to the critical mass of any group, adaption is one of the strategies taken by the nondominant groups.

Indirect and direct ways of speaking can be found between languages also. Consider that Japanese or Indian dialects might have speech patterns that sound more indirect than English does. Yet, as I previously stated, I have asked people all over the world whether they experience women and men speaking differently. So far, every person has responded that they do indeed detect differences. There may be differences between cultures and languages, but within any given language, there usually will be a gender difference.

These indirect and direct speaking styles can be a hazard in the diverse workplace. Consider the following scenario, exaggerated a bit: A woman approaches her assistant and asks her to do something. "Could you possibly do this by 5:00 P.M.? I know how busy you are and I don't want to bother you because what you are doing right now is quite important, and you are a strong part of this team. I would greatly appreciate it if you could. What do you think?" This is clearly an example of indirect speech. Nothing is right or wrong about it. But in Noah's ark? Let's say the woman's male manager overhears her talking to the assistant. He may unconsciously be wondering why this woman can't just get to the point. He wonders why she is essentially begging her assistant to do something. And it seems to the manager that the woman isn't being clear about the fact that she *does* need the report by 5:00 P.M., so she also appears to be wasting time. Furthermore, if this manager is responsible for evaluating the woman, he might see this exchange as an example of how she lacks the ability to manage. He will likely criticize her approach and speaking style because it is not his ritual way of interacting. He may deem her a poor manager and confirm in his mind that this is evidence of her inability to lead. He writes that in her performance evaluation, and discourages promoting her.

So—how might he have spoken to the assistant? The male might have instead said something like, "I need this by 5:00 P.M."; or, if highly emotionally intelligent, "*Please* do this by 5:00 P.M." Most men would say it in a simple and succinct manner; but here again is the Noah's ark problem. If this man's manager is a woman, and she hears him talk to the assistant like that, she may think that this man is rude, has no emotional intelligence, and does not know how to motivate people and make them feel part of the team. He just orders people around, which seems to her to be a terrible way to supervise others. In her mind, this method of leading shows no relationship skills whatsoever. She would in turn be likely to rate the male as a bad people manager, because this is not how Grandma taught her to speak to others.

Here we have each manager, male and female, negatively evaluating the person who handles a situation in a way that is different from how they would have acted or spoken. It differs from the way each of them was taught by their own Grandma to speak to others. Neither way is right or wrong; it just appears that way to the opposite speaker. The playing field has become unleveled for both parties, because of the fact that each manager has just made an inaccurate evaluation based on speaking styles and based on their own rituals and comfort zones.

There is another interesting phenomenon at play here. Imagine what would happen if the woman went up to the assistant and abruptly said, "I need this done by 5:00 P.M." In this example, the woman would have adopted a more *male* style of managing—and she would likely pay the price. In these instances, we hear people call a woman a bitch, or say that she is too aggressive. And to be fair—if the man started using indirect language such as, "if you wouldn't mind," or, "if it isn't too much trouble," he'd likely be labeled a pushover or wimp. Sociologists call this "cognitive dissonance with resulting blowback." Each individual has crossed over and taken on the archetype rituals of the other. In turn, people don't know how to react—or they react negatively—when people get out of their expected role behaviors.

These are what I call the "terrible too's." I often warn managers who review employees to be cognizant of calling someone "too" something—such as too aggressive, too assertive, or too emotional. It's typically a signal that the employee being evaluated has stepped out of their expected role, and spoken or acted like the other; often it means that the manager is uneasy with the behavior based on his or her own Grandma's teachings. Calling an employee too anything is usually just an unconscious way of evaluating someone who isn't acting as you expected. It is important for the manager to assess whether the employee is *really* demonstrating inappropriate aggressiveness, or whether a woman just happens to be more direct than expected—in which case, she isn't actually causing a problem. Maybe she is just too assertive for *him*.

Litmus Test

If you hear a woman giving instructions that you deem appropriate and hear a man give the same instructions in the same language style but consider it weak and unhelpful, then it's important to evaluate why. If you automatically react negatively to the man's indirect style but not the woman's, then you have created an unleveled playing field, eroded the meritocracy, and mismanaged Noah's ark in such a way that will ensure that diversity is not working. And this ritual speaking paradox is not just found along gender lines; we might think badly of *anyone* who speaks in a different customary style than we do.

Another example of how this indirect/direct perception crops up is how a woman presents an idea as compared to how a man presents the same idea at a meeting. Let's say that the woman, Susan, says, "I am thinking we might want to consider Plan A, although it could be possible to think about Plan B. But I would like to hear everyone's ideas about Plan C." And then none of the men in the room offer comments on her idea. Michael, the male presenter, says, "We need to go with Plan A, B, or C." The other men nod in agreement, and tell Michael he has some good ideas. The women are looking around the room befuddled, because they heard Susan say the exact same thing. The men either didn't hear it, or thought Susan hadn't thoroughly solidified her ideas. Although the males in the room heard some concepts being tossed around, they didn't hear Susan clearly recommending anything specific to the group.

Not giving equal weight to contributions based on who makes comments and the style of speaking is a subtle inequity. I once saw a cartoon with four men and one woman sitting in a meeting. The caption read, "Miss Smith, would you like one of the men to say what you just said so the other men will hear it?"

What follows from that is the potential for an unleveled playing field—one in which credit is given to the wrong person. Herein lies the essence of the Noah's ark conundrum. If a male manager is evaluating Michael on his presentation, he is likely to have heard clearly articulated ideas and witnessed other men affirming those ideas. The manager makes a mental note about what a good contribution Michael made to the discussion. This ends up in the pile of mental and written notes that influence Michael's review, promotion, and salary. This same manager fails to see how Susan has added to the meeting, doesn't give her any credit for her contribution, and in turn, Susan ends up being incredibly frustrated.

The reverse can occur as well. If the evaluating manager is a woman, most likely she heard Susan quite clearly, and did not find anything indecisive about her presentation. This same manager listens to Michael and observes that, once again, he seems to be taking another colleague's ideas and trying to get credit for them. And while Michael certainly isn't doing this, the female manager has another way of interpreting the presentation. The potential is equally great for the woman manager to view Michael's presentation only through her own lens.

Indirect speaking, which is often seen in other linguistic styles, tends to signal that you are inviting others into the conversation. In essence, it is a way of saying, "I would like to hear what others are thinking." Listeners feel that the discussion is open in such a situation. Direct speaking, on the other hand, is good for giving orders. If the building is burning, for example, you don't want to convey the sentiment that, "I am thinking we should go out door A, but I would like to hear what others think about door B." It's imperative that someone say, "Go out door A now" without hesitation.

Women tend to speak with ritual questions and apologies, and with substantial concern for being considerate and caring (or at least appearing to be so). These ritual questions are relational ways not to sound like someone is being *ordered* to do something. But the ritual question is also a means of making a statement or giving an order. Take, for example, a man and woman who are in a car together. The man is driving, and the woman says, "Do you want to stop for lunch?" The man, who is a direct speaker and thinks he just heard a question, ponders for a moment, and says, "No." The woman is furious. She had just said that she wanted to stop for lunch, and is now frustrated that the man didn't hear that. Had she been with another woman and asked that same question, either the other woman would have known immediately that the questioner was saying she wanted to stop for lunch, or she would have responded with other ritual questions such as, "No, I don't want to stop, but do you?"

After relaying the above scenario to a group of executives, one of the men in the group said he could relate to these ritual questions. A friend of his had gone out on a first date that had gone very well. At the end of the evening, the woman said to his friend, "Do you want to come up for a cup of coffee?" The friend apparently responded, "No, I don't drink coffee." Coffee or not, we can see how the woman was inviting the man to continue their date, whereas the man was answering directly to the offer of coffee, which he didn't want. This is the classic difference between a relational comment and a transactional one—as well as fodder for a Jerry Seinfeld comedy act.

Direct and indirect deferential speaking patterns often occur within power dynamics, and can be misinterpreted across cultural differences as well. In his book *Outliers*, Malcolm Gladwell relates a tragic example of this when an airline pilot defers to the captain (because culturally, the captain is more powerful), does not contradict the captain, speaks indirectly about a malfunction, and ends up in a horrific plane crash. This pattern was reported in the case of the 1982 Air Florida tragedy—a situation in which the wings needed deicing in winter. The analysis of the crash later showed that the captain maintained an image of not needing advice, while the copilot and other less powerful individuals were afraid to assert themselves. It was a textbook example of power dynamics and of failing to understand how the other communicates and listens. The less powerful have to be trained to be more assertive and to speak consciously and directly to the perceived more powerful captain; the more powerful need to listen bilingually to the other's speech patterns.

The best leaders will find a way to be conscious of and to use both the tools of indirect and direct speech, depending on the circumstances. In other words, they will adopt the most enviable traits of both the direct and indirect speaker, which often correlates to the styles of the dominant and nondominant groups—depending on the need, the audience, and the situation.

I like the frame in which consultant Michael Johnson, founder of Diamond Dynamics, puts this difference of the genders. He studied the Girl Scout and Boy Scout mottos. The Girl Scouts promise that they will be friendly, helpful, considerate and caring, make the world a better place, and be a sister. The Boy Scouts promise to keep themselves physically strong, be true to family, scouts, school and nation, not hurt or kill harmless things (without reason), be obedient and follow the rules, be thrifty, pay their own way and help others, be brave, face danger even if afraid, have courage, and be prepared. Quite a different frame of view for behaving that Grandma taught boys and girls.

In organizations, managers have the power to allocate scarce resources, hire, fire, promote, judge, review, give raises, and assign good projects. The employees receive these positive and negative experiences based on the norms of the culture and how closely they ascribe to them. In diverse organizations, the dynamics are complex. We often evaluate the advantage or disadvantage of others based on those we are comfortable with, and whether their speaking rituals sound like our own. It helps, then, if two people bring the same Grandmas to work, but that is precisely what *doesn't* happen with diversity. We unconsciously have right and wrong columns in our head that we add up. When we put different people together—which diversity inherently does—we have to go the next step, move beyond the diversity, and be conscious of who we and others are. Only then can we get the true value of that diversity, make the workplace fair, keep the pipelines flowing, and have more effective global companies.

Chapter 7

The Tools in Your Toolbox

"To the man who only has a hammer in the toolkit, every problem looks like a nail"—so said renowned humanistic psychologist Abraham Maslow. In much the same way, it is essential that leaders, managers, and employees focus on building and establishing the appropriate tools needed to turn their work environments into a truly diverse, cognitively rich meritocracy—with fairness and a level playing field for everyone aboard the ark. Using that approach, we can avoid the traps of diversity, and decode some of the unconscious cloaked behaviors. There is a way to find the tools that are necessary, discover a different way of managing, or uncover a new method of expressing yourself that ends up being more productive. In other words, we can—with enough deliberate thought and practice—find more than just hammers in our toolboxes.

The more tools each of us has to work with, the better off our end product will be, and the more success we will have with diversity. To have only a hammer or a screwdriver makes you less able to do any sophisticated management or career advancing—what you also need are a wrench, a dowel, a level, and tape measure. In any organization, the responsibility for making the corporate Noah's ark a success rests with both tools of the individual *and* the institution.

Members of the management team represent the institutional culture and style, and as I have emphasized, each manager has a *playing field*, or an area of responsibility within the organization. If all managers' sections were combined, the result would be the institution's total playing field. And with the way things work in diverse corporate cultures today, it is practically guaranteed that no one's playing field is entirely level. I'm not suggesting that people are malicious or biased, nor do I think they intend on making an organization unfair. But as long as institutions continue to maintain unleveled playing fields—and because of the hidden effects of diversity—responsibility almost always falls to the individual to somehow fix or navigate the broken system.

On the other hand, many employees rely solely upon the institution—when in reality, they could also identify small changes they could make individually, while adding a few of their own tools to the situation. Some team members expect management to do all of the outreach and heavy lifting for them, and assume that this is not part of their job description. As far as I'm concerned, the responsibility rests with both. Take the example discussed earlier of interruptions at a meeting. A manager needs to be aware of the dynamics that lurk underneath, and be especially sensitive to who has an inclination to interrupt and dominate versus who *naturally* remains quiet and unheard. It is important that a manager have the tool of awareness so that she can take an affirmative step to level the cultural playing field. The manager must watch what is happening, pick up a new tool, and say as I suggested before, "Hold on John, let Ming finish his thought," or, "Let's hear from Prakash first." Similarly, a particular member of the organization might want to observe his or her own natural behavior, consider how it may affect others, and pick up a new tool as well. Individuals should step up and refuse to let their colleagues interrupt or keep them silent—even if their Grandma taught them to stop talking or keep quiet.

When it comes to asking for a raise or promotion, women and other nondominant groups often hesitate to assert themselves. There are many reasons for this, but the important area to focus on is the result. Ultimately, raises and promotions are likely to go disproportionately to those who ask for them—those who speak up. An individual may need to develop tools that enable them to tell their manager what they are doing; to develop ways to promote their work; and to state specifically their career goals.

Simultaneously, the manager must develop a keen sense of awareness within the corporate Noah's ark. He or she must understand what results—even unintentionally—when those who speak up are rewarded, and those who don't are the ones who lose out. A good manager will take it upon himself to solicit information from his diverse employees. He should be asking individuals about their career goals and considering pay based on merit, not on whether someone was a constant presence in their office or was at the gym with them.

This is not about rigid adherence to a particular approach, and it isn't the organization saying, "Be like me." Style compliance is exhausting if you are the one always forcing yourself to bend to the dominant style. As we've seen, the way we approach work is very rooted in how we approach life—which we learn fundamentally through the lens of our own background, culture, norms, parents, movies, and myths. This is what diversity brings, and it creates unintended consequences.

None of us come with the *wrong* approach, of course. However, some of us get lucky—especially if our approach just happens to be the one most valued by the organization. We are fortunate if we happen to fit in with the dominant style; we start off with an advantage this way. The tools these individuals have brought with them to work seem to be just the right ones. They fit in with relative ease, and find success with little awareness of the privilege that comes with it. Style acceptance usually comes when the group has a critical mass in the organization.

But it may not come as easily to others. They bring tools in to work, as well, but they find that theirs may not always work well, even though the value of diversity is supposed to mean a mixing and adding of tools. In fact, these minority groups may bring different—but even more useful—tools to fix the complex problems that diverse global organizations face. The point is that everybody in a culturally varied work environment brings a limited set of tools—and not the same set. We can all benefit from adding our own toolboxes to the mix, and finding solutions based on everything that has been brought to the table.

Let's look more closely at a few tools that can help create a level playing field, a more profitable global corporation, and more successful employees.

THINK ABOUT THE PEOPLE ON YOUR TEAM

If You Are a Manager: Are you planning activities that actually include *everyone* on the team? I recently spoke to a diverse group of managers, one of whom was excited to tell about a team activity that he had started to increase morale and bring people together. "Great," I said, "What is it?" He told me that he planned gatherings and activities around "March Madness." I then asked a number of the women in the room if they knew or cared about March Madness—the college basketball championship series—and while a few did, most hadn't heard of it or didn't really care about it. The Koreans, Indians, and Brazilians in the room were even less familiar with March Madness. Although he hadn't meant to exclude anyone, this manager was bonding with people just like him—people who knew and liked basketball. He therefore spent a disproportionate amount of time with those colleagues, while the other diverse team members were left out.

"Let's get lunch." A seemingly innocuous invitation by a manager can actually create disproportionate access for some and a loss of similar access to others if the manager only goes with those she can relax with or trust.

If You Are an Employee: To start, if you find yourself not having the same access or opportunity to bond with your manager, find ways in which both of you can get to know each other informally. Suppress Grandma's whispering about bothering the manager or wasting their time with your chitchat. Also, allow the manager the opportunity to walk in your shoes by suggesting a few more inclusive activities.

LEARN TO RECOGNIZE OTHER PEOPLE'S "GRANDMAS"

Every one of us experiences life in a distinct way, and this is especially true for groups that are either dominant or non-dominant. For U.S. companies, women, minorities, non-Americans, and others working in a dominant culture will experience an organization substantially differently than those who have historically held power. It's important for managers to recognize these subtle and not so subtle differences, and adjust accordingly. This may mean that a manager has to force herself out of her own comfort zone in order to watch, observe, and accommodate nondominant individuals. Remaining sensitive to and aware of the fact that not everyone comes from the same place or uses the same frame of reference is an important tool.

If You Are a Manager: Ask, listen, and be aware. Notice the different ways in which members of your team are experiencing the world of work and all its dynamics. Who is speaking more than listening? Who listens more often than talks? Who speaks differently than you? How do you give feedback to people who are not like you, or who *are* like you? What are your real concerns and how does that change your message to employees who are not like you?

If You Are an Employee: Remember that remaining silent is not a successful strategy. Find ways to let your manager know about the world in which you live. In that focus group that I conducted at my previous company, it became clear to me that the dominant group—or the white American men—did have some sense of the experiences that the non-Americans were having. They might understand the limitations of heading up the Taiwan office and then trying to move to head up the Dallas corporate office. They had a slight understanding of what women experienced, but they had almost *no* understanding of the world the minorities lived in. This was partly because there are often fewer opportunities outside of work to share life's daily experiences. Few white American men go to the weddings, churches, and neighborhoods of their Latino colleagues. So try to reach out and introduce more people to your world.

FAIR AND EQUAL WITH ACCESS, KNOWLEDGE, AND FEEDBACK

If You Are a Manager: Access to a manager is a valuable commodity, since a manager will often unconsciously give the benefits he or she has to offer to the person with whom they are most familiar and comfortable. While it is fine to play basketball with your employees and colleagues, be conscious of the fact that spending hours outside of the office with certain people means you will naturally get to know them well — while *not* getting to know the other members of your team. You will feel comfortable with your sports buddies, and when the next opportunity comes up, you may be inclined to put that companion forward for a promotion — possibly over someone better qualified whom you know less well, or with whom you have fewer common bonds. To keep the playing field level, the skilled manager needs to find ways to learn about the other members of the team so that an equal level of comfort and knowledge exists with the people who aren't naturally like you. There may even be many more unfamiliar faces than there are familiar ones in Noah's ark.

This goes for the subtle process that takes place when an individual employee tells her manager what she is doing, states her accomplishments, and receives feedback. Even if you think you have little to say, it is often enough to state during a meeting, "Mike, I'm really behind what you just said."

As we have seen in a diverse workplace, these elements are often unevenly handled. My simple tool for solving this problem is for the manager to require that everyone regularly let him or her know what they have accomplished, or think they are doing well, and for the manager to tell individuals consistently what they need to work on. I emphasize the word *consistent*, because an annual comment and feedback session doesn't solve this problem. Meeting once a year is not frequent enough to overcome the awkwardness that often exists between two unlike people. Frequency is the key here, and getting together once a month or bimonthly can lower barriers and reset habits brought in from cultural, gender, and other differences.

I remember when my reserve police partner initially gave me feedback. He's a very direct speaker, and so the first time he let me know how he thought I was doing, I almost hit him. He said, "Laura, you are such an idiot." "What did you just say to me?" I thought, feeling rather irate. He was concerned about how I walked up to a car and stuck my hand into it—a potentially dangerous action.

Over time—and because we work together frequently—I have come to realize that this manner of giving feedback is simply his way of showing concern about me. He doesn't want anything to happen to me. But his very direct criticism required some getting used to; and it took me some time to understand his message.

If You Are an Employee: Realize that you do not need to play bridge, basketball, golf, ski, or go to the pub in order to advance at work. However, you should consider the issue of *access*. Make sure that you create access opportunities for you and your manager. It might feel a little uncomfortable at first, because you may be battling with a Grandma who taught you not to inconvenience someone who's higher up on the corporate ladder than you are. Set up a regular time to meet, write, or communicate what you are doing, and ask your manager to tell you regularly how you might improve. Remember—you are not *bothering* your supervisor; you are merely going after what others in the ark are already being given. You have a responsibility to yourself to get to that same level of comfort, and more importantly, valuable information and exchange with your manager.

BE CAREFUL WITH YOUR WORDS, AND HOW YOU INTERPRET THE WORDS OF OTHERS

We all may speak a common language in an organization; however, that doesn't mean that we all communicate or respond in the same way. In Noah's ark, *too* and *not enough* are rarely productive words to use. "She's too aggressive" or "too emotional," or, "He's not assertive enough" may be more about your reaction than their behavior. Too and not enough are evaluative words that are usually based on our own perceptions of how people should behave—and the archetypes we carry within us. And they won't actually help to accomplish your goals. More often than not, these words create confusion or resentment rather than offering motivation, encouragement, or constructive criticism.

We often react to the expected speech patterns and norms that we have heard growing up—whether they're from the other gender, or from the hierarchies of status within a society. We expect a woman to speak a certain way, or a lower-level employee to speak in a pattern of style when addressing a superior. When these groups don't act as expected, we tend to react negatively. Similarly, what we might find perfectly acceptable in a man we sometimes find quite jarring coming from a woman. While we're in the bar scene or a social environment, that may be just fine. But in Noah's ark, we have the power to promote, demote, hire, fire, and pay—and these subtle reactions can add up to severe damage to a person based on our own unconscious reactions to their style.

The litmus test can always be used. As a manager, am I perfectly content when a British man who works for me casually interrupts me in the office, talks about what he has done, and invites me for a drink after work? How do I react if the Chinese woman who works for me sticks her head in the door, asks for a minute of my time, brags about the deal she just did, and invites me to play golf with her on the weekend? We have to consider why we probably wouldn't react the same way to each of these scenarios. It is *not* the diversity that is the problem—it is our unconscious, Grandma-based learning about difference that is causing the unfair reaction.

THE SILENT HAVE SOMETHING TO SAY

We worked hard, spent a lot of money, and dedicated much time to our goal of diversity in our organizations. We want different ideas, perspectives, worldviews, and cognitive diversity. Yet so often, there is still silence coming from many members of our team—not because the quiet employees are lacking ideas, but because there are dynamics playing out under the surface. Either a manager notices this, or they don't. If your managers aren't noticing, then there is no sense in spending another dime on diversity efforts—because they won't pay off.

If You Are a Manager: In meetings, it is essential to be conscious of who is speaking and how often everyone shares their opinions. Allow time for every member of the team to be able to talk in meetings, and keep an open-door policy so that they can speak to you candidly if necessary. In order to ensure that everyone is heard, you may have to call on people directly, or politely ask that someone wait their turn. Conference calls are a particularly fertile breeding ground for silence.

If You Are an Employee: If you do not speak, your ideas will not be heard. It is that simple. The act of speaking up is not an easy one for some, but you can't blame it all on Grandma. You have a responsibility to participate and share your ideas. Otherwise, you will have to accept that you are creating a work environment that isn't fair for you. Ask your manager to allow you to speak in the meeting or the conference. Advise him or her that you would like to be the first person to present at the meeting this time. Help your colleagues by noticing if someone is remaining silent in a meeting and ask them what they are thinking, even if the manager does not.

RESULTS SHOULD BE THE DETERMINANT

We are often so wrapped up in how someone spoke that we forget that there are results that can be measured. Even if you would not speak the way someone else does, or might handle the team differently, look at the results to see if the company is getting what it needs. In Noah's ark, there are many undercurrents at work—a mélange of approaches, habits, communication styles, and rituals of words or actions. We know our own, and we think they are the right ones. Yet diversity forces us to work harder to understand that many different approaches can bring better outcomes.

Diversity consultant Kendall Wright often asks employees to participate in an exercise in which he asks groups of individuals how they each mathematically arrive at the number 100. As is quickly discovered, there are myriad ways to do so—10 times 10, 1 times 100, 200 divided by 2, 50 + 50. You get the point. The more ways to approach our goals, the better decisions can be made. If you rely upon your default ways, then the organization is limited in its creativity, and you are limited in your success.

CONCLUSION

It is by no means easy to create a successful Noah's ark of diversity, yet once accomplished—and with much sustained consciousness—the rewards are enormous. I honestly believe that just being conscious is half the battle. Once you—as an employee or a leader—are aware of the pitfalls, the glories, the tools, and the differences, you'll never go backward. You won't revert to your former ways of seeing things.

Much well-intentioned effort is spent on moves toward corporate diversity, yet we have not done what I call hurry history. Research from organizations like Catalyst, Ernst and Young, McKinsey, and the World Economic Forum all point to the fact that there are still many holes in the pipeline. The pyramid of the corporation still has too many of some types at the bottom and too many of other types at the top. Often, the research is focused on women or racial minorities, but as we have seen, Noah's ark brings all kinds into the organization. If we looked more closely, we might find that as a percentage, there are more golfers at the top, and fewer at the bottom.

Through thoughtfully run meetings, postwork activities, mentoring, feedback, promotions, career development, evaluations, individual communication interactions, other corporate processes—the culture can, and *must* go beyond accepting, tolerating, including, and referencing diversity. We must understand the dynamics of dominant and nondominant, subtle actions, unwritten rules, unconscious perceptions, and how we each walk in the world. Corporations can take all of the norms that Grandma gave all of their employees and create a new norm—one that focuses on deliberately and consciously doing business in a diverse global environment, creating a truly leveled playing field, and reaping the rewards of what we all bring to the workplace. This is how we embrace our difference, move beyond diversity, and become more successful than ever before. From now on I hope you will notice the Wheel, the Duck, the Nail, and the Nice.

References

Books

Babcock, Linda, and Sara Laschever. 2007. *Women Don't Ask: Negotiation and the Gender Divide*. New York: Bantam Dell.

Bateson, Mary Catherine. 2001. *Composing a Life*. New York: Grove Press.

Fels, Anna. 2004. *Necessary Dreams: Ambition in Women's Changing Lives*. New York: Pantheon Books.

Fox, Richard, 2005. *It Takes a Candidate: Why Women Don't Run for Office*, Cambridge University Press.

Gardner, Howard, and Emma Laskin. 1996. *Leading Minds: An Anatomy of Leadership*. New York: BasicBooks.

Gladwell, Malcolm. 2005. *Blink: The Power of Thinking Without Thinking*. New York: Little, Brown and Company.

Gladwell, Malcolm. 2008. *Outliers: The Story of Success*. New York: Little, Brown and Company.

Jamieson, Kathleen Hall. 1995. *Beyond the Double Bind: Women and Leadership*. Oxford University Press.

Liswood, Laura A. 1996, 2009. *Women World Leaders*. New York: HarperCollins.

Page, Scott E. 2007. *The Difference: How the Power of Diversity Creates Better Groups, Firms, Schools and Societies*. Princeton: Princeton University Press.

151

Surowiecki, James. 2004. *The Wisdom of Crowds*. New York: Random House.

Tannen, Deborah. 1994. *Talking from 9 to 5: Women and Men at Work*. New York: HarperCollins. New York: First Quill, 2001.

Tannen, Deborah. 1999. *You Just Don't Understand: Women and Men in Conversation*. New York: Ballantine. New York: First Quill, 2001.

Thompson, George J., and Jerry B. Jenkins. 2004. *Verbal Judo: The Gentle Art of Persuasion*. New York: HarperCollins.

Tavris, Carol, and Elliot Aronson. 2007. *Mistakes were Made (but not by me): Why we Justify Foolish Beliefs, Bad Decisions, and Hurtful Acts*. Orlando: Harcourt Press.

Periodicals, Journals, and Research Reports

Baron, A. S., & M. R. Banaji. Implicit association test. *Encyclopedia of Intergroup Relations*.

Begley, Sharon. 2006. He, once a she, offers own view on science spat. *Wall Street Journal*, July 13.

Brescoll, Victoria. 2008. Can an Angry Woman Get Ahead? Gender, Status Conferral, and Workplace Emotion Expression, *Psychological Science*.

Funderburg, Lisa. 2005. The little chill. *O Magazine*, November: 266.

Goldin, Claudia, and Cecilia Rouse. 2000. Orchestrating impartiality: The impact of "blind" auditions on female musicians. *American Economic*, September: 715–741.

Goudreau, Jenna, Marjorie Backman, and Leah McGrath Goodman. 2008. Business: The anger effect. *ForbesLife Executive Woman*, November: 14.

Hausmann, Richard, Laura Tyson, and Saada Zahidi. The global gender gap report. *World Economic Forum*, 2006, 2007, and 2008 editions.

Hewlett, Sylvia Ann, and Carolyn Buck Luce. 2005. Off-ramps and on-ramps. *Harvard Business Review*, March.

Holland, Kelley. 2006. The silent may have something to say. *New York Times*, November 5.

Joyce, Amy. 2007. Her pay gap begins right after graduation. *Washington Post*, April 29.

Liswood, Laura. 2009. Where would we be if women ran Wall Street? *International Herald Tribune*, February 2.

Mark, Marilyn. 2001. Blind auditions key to hiring musicians. *Princeton Weekly Bulletin*, February 12.

Rowe, Mary P. 1990. Barriers to equality: The power of subtle discrimination to maintain unequal opportunity. *Employee Responsibilities and Rights Journal*, 3.2.

Tannen, Deborah. 1995. Power of talk: Who gets heard and why. *Harvard Business Review*, September/October.

Thomas, David. 2001. The truth about mentoring minorities: Race matters. *Harvard Business Review*, April.

Young, Steve. 2001. Micro-inequities: The power of small. *Profiles in Diversity Journal*, September.

Wilbur, Del Quentin. 2007. A crash's improbable impact. *Washington Post*, January 12.

Other Resources

American Council on Education

Beth Brooke, Vice Chairman, Ernst and Young, New York, NY

Center for American Woman and Politics, Rutgers University

Equal Employment Opportunity Commission (EEOC)

Linda Hill, Wallace Brett Donham Professor of Business Administration. Harvard Business School, Cambridge, MA

Michael Johnson, Diamond Dynamics, Watsonville, CA

Ilene Lang, President and CEO. Catalyst Inc., New York, NY

Massachusetts Institute of Technology (MIT)

Kendall C. Wright, Diversity Expert. Entelechy Training and Development. West Chester, OH

Saadia Zaadia, the Women Leadership Programme, World Economic Forum, Geneva, Switzerland

Interviews

Excerpts of edited transcripts of interviews with the following people are available at www.theloudestduck .com.

Cherie Blair, barrister, spouse of former British Prime Minister Tony Blair

Christine Di Stefano, political science professor, University of Washington

David Gergen, presidential advisor, *CNN* commentator, dean of Harvard Kennedy School of Government Leadership Center

Gwen Ifil, managing editor *Washington Week* and senior correspondent *The NewsHour with Jim Lehrer*

Janet Napolitano, secretary of Homeland Security, former governor of Arizona

Joseph S. Nye, Jr., professor, Harvard Kennedy School of Government, former dean of HKS

Pepper Schwartz, professor, University of Washington, sociologist and author

Ellen Johnson-Sirleaf, president of Liberia

Laura Tyson, professor, economic advisor, former dean, London School of Business

Heather Wilson, security expert, former U.S. Representative, New Mexico

Web Sites

www.theloudestduck.com

www.lauraliswood.com

Index